American Catholic Leadership:
A Decade of Turmoil

Religion and Society 11

GENERAL EDITORS

Leo Laeyendecker, *University of Leyden*
Jacques Waardenburg, *University of Utrecht*

MOUTON PUBLISHERS · THE HAGUE · PARIS · NEW YORK

American Catholic Leadership: A Decade of Turmoil 1966–1976

A Sociological Analysis of the National Federation of Priests' Councils

JAMES H. STEWART

Saint Olaf College
Northfield, Minnesota

MOUTON PUBLISHERS · THE HAGUE · PARIS · NEW YORK

ISBN: 90–279–7884–0

© 1978, Mouton Publishers, The Hague, The Netherlands

Printed in Great Britain

For my wife, Lu, and children, Chris and Patch

Foreword

by
ANDREW M. GREELEY

The changes in the Catholic Church between the convening of the Second Vatican Council in the early 1960s and the present time constitute one of the most fascinating fields for research in the sociology of religion and the sociology of organization ever made available to social researchers. An organization that seemed immutable suddenly, or so it seemed, went through dramatic and then traumatic change—perhaps the most dramatic change to have affected it in more than one thousand years. As a result of the change, or so it seemed, there were massive resignations from the priesthood and religious life and notable declines (in the United States, at any rate) on most measures of religious behavior. (Although recent research has suggested that as far as the laity are concerned at least, the conciliar changes were extremely successful and that other events, most notably the issuance of the birth control encyclical *Humanae Vitae*, account for the decline in devotional practices.)

Professor Stewart has chosen one aspect of the change for his examination under the scholar's microscope, the emergence of a professional association, perhaps even a union, of Roman Catholic priests. It is one of the merits of his work that he is able to combine sympathy with discretion and objectivity. One does not have to read very far into the volume to tell that Professor Stewart is reporting from the inside, that he is a committed 'postconciliar' Roman Catholic, and that his own personal religious and social positions are quite close to those held by those who have emerged as the ruling elite of the National Federation of Priests' Councils. But he is still able to maintain the strict objectivity of the professional social scientist in reporting the ambiguities, the mistakes, the frustrations, and the uncertainties that faced and still face the NFPC. I suspect that the NFPC leadership will be pleased by many parts of this volume; they will also find many parts make painful reading.

Professor Stewart closes on a somewhat hopeful note. He seems to be reasonably optimistic about the future of the NFPC. I would be inclined to be more reserved, perhaps because I have little faith in the NFPC leadership. I quit the Chicago constituent group when Patrick O'Malley, then president of the NFPC, demanded that I turn over the data from the NORC priesthood study to a sociologist he would designate on the grounds that I was studying the priesthood 'from the bishops' viewpoint' and he wanted someone to study it from the priests' viewpoint. When I failed to accede to his ultimatum, Father O'Malley commissioned another study, apparently to 'refute' ours. One doesn't pay due to those who question your honesty and integrity.

The NFPC, in my judgment, reflects some of the fundamental problems of the presbyterate that it is attempting to represent organizationally: it has little respect for and little understanding of professional scholarly competence, and it is permeated by the envy of mediocre men for those who dare to step too far beyond the boundaries of the established clerical culture. Certainly the NFPC is more politically and socially progressive than the presbyterate it represents, but one can expect the NFPC to go beyond envy and mediocrity only when the presbyterate moves beyond it. My hunch is that such a movement will take place not because of what takes place within the priesthood but because of the reform of the American church on high that is currently being accomplished by the transformation of the American hierarchy under the leadership of the present apostolic delegate Jean Jadot. Ironically, the priesthood will be transformed not because of its own professional organization but because of a Rome-appointed apostolic delegate and the new bishops he has brought to church leadership.

I imagine that Professor Stewart will find this judgment of the NFPC made from inside the presbyterate somewhat at odds with his own much more sympathetic judgment made from the outside. However, I do not think there is a basic disharmony between the two. As a priest, I guess I expected far more of the NFPC than they were able to produce; perhaps, as a lay person, Professor Stewart expected far less. Fair enough.

It must be said in all fairness to the NFPC that in some respects it reflects the strength and assets of the American presbyterate. It has been flexible, pragmatic (at least relatively so), and ingenious in evolving an open-ended organizational structure. I doubt that priests in many other countries could organize so well and so effectively. Perhaps the most serious organizational blows to the NFPC have been the resignations from the priesthood of some of its top leadership. These have been serious blows to the organization's credibility it is much to be feared.

I am surprised that as a layman Professor Stewart is not more concerned about the NFPC's failure to face seriously some of the most important ministerial problems that the laity encounter in their experience with the clergy. Surely the most powerful dissatisfaction among the laity with clerical performance has to do with the quality of preaching. And yet the NFPC has made little if any effort to improve the professional performance of the presbyterate in this area. I have the impression that so much of their time was spent trying to dialogue with bishops on the rights of priests *vis-à-vis* the hierarchy that there was little time left to dialogue with the rank and file laity on the subject of their rights *vis-à-vis* the clergy— especially the right to hear a decent Sunday sermon.

Again, my difference with Professor Stewart is probably one of a matter of emphasis. He is pleased with the professional association of priests that came into existence in a short period of time, consolidated its existence, and began to build toward the future; I am dissatisfied because the organization has not turned its attention to preaching. I must say in all candor that Professor Stewart's expectations are more reasonable than mine and better represent the realistic expectations of a social scientist. He has advanced our understanding of the American priesthood and the Catholic Church in transition. He appears to be more hopeful about the prospects of the NFPC's future than I am. I hope he is right.

Foreword

by

R. D. JAMES RATIGAN

President of the NFPC

When, on January 25, 1959, Pope John XXIII made his unexpected announcement of his plan to convoke the Catholic Church's twenty-first Ecumenical Council, he chided the prophets of doom within the Church. The prophets of doom were wrong then, and they are wrong today. Vatican Council II set a new agenda for the Catholic Church.

The majority of priests in the United States, by training and also by cultural and ethnic background, are men of structures. It is no wonder, then, that their response to the demands of Vatican II was to establish organizations and structures to meet the new challenge.

Those first days were times of tensions and of growth. Power structures of decision making, which had functioned one way for centuries, were being asked to change. For both priests and bishops this was a new experience. The short experience of 1966 and a portion of 1967 in priest organization moved some priests to respond to a need for collaboration on a national level. Their ultimate goal was to build a Church in which the priests were more responsive to the needs of the people. Within its short history, the National Federation of Priests' Councils has kept close ties with its grassroots work while, at the same time, building collaborative efforts and coalitions with the National Conference of Catholic Bishops and other national Catholic organizations.

As priests are called ever more to creative styles of leadership in ministry, the local council and the national federation are needed both to challenge and to support the efforts of priests. The 1977 Call to Action Conference, convened by the Bishops' Committee for the Bicentennial, is testimony that the people want the Church continually to address the needs of the world with a new and creative response. The short history of the federation has demonstrated that the local priests' councils, who make up the federation, have been willing to meet that challenge in the past and have both the will and the ability to continue to do so.

The federation can look with pride to its accomplishments: due process procedures in most dioceses, personnel boards and policies, prayer symposia, rural ministry workshops, a new selection of bishops process, a voice for the establishment of other important national organizations: National Organization for the Continuing Education of Roman Catholic Clergy, Inc., National Association of Church Personnel Administrators, and National Catholic Coalition for Responsible Investment.

Too often movements and organizations can go for long periods of time without the benefit of critical analysis. For that reason the National Federation of Priests' Councils is grateful to Doctor Stewart for his informed and insightful analysis. It will provide an effective tool for our own self-understanding, as well as an opportunity for others in the Church to become better acquainted with the far-reaching and critical work of the federation.

The 1976 NFPC House of Delegates affirmed their belief that all men and women within the Church are called in equal dignity to minister. In the coming years the role of the federation will be to listen not only to the priests in the member councils, but to all ministers, to collaborate and to support those who continue to challenge the Church to be true to its hopes and its promises.

Author's Preface

In 1968 the National Federation of Priests' Councils was born in travail. This was the time when the U.S. Catholic Church was experiencing a malaise and turmoil which stemmed from the shock waves of Vatican II as well as the cultural and social upheaval during the 1960s. The NFPC began without sanction of the Catholic bishops.

To launch an autonomous national federation of organized groups of priests was a radically new idea. It was also a sociological miracle in that the more moderate senates of 1968 were willing to join liberal free associations of priests in constituting a social movement of priests.

Besides being a new idea and a social miracle, it was deviant and illegitimate. The initial agenda for change, dealing first of all with the problem of priests' 'interests' issues and secondly with 'value' issues found in the pastoral and social ministry, forced the federation into controversy. Many if not most of the bishops judged it as an enemy's camp threatening their authority and official prerogatives. During its first four years of existence, it was indeed a thorn in the side of the NCCB.

Beginning in 1973 and by 1977, however, the NFPC and the bishops were at least cooperating with each other on an unofficial level. But formal recognition of the NFPC has yet to come. 'Interest' issues and confrontration tactics had crested with the 'Moment of Truth' statement and by the 1972 convention in Denver, the federation began shifting gears moving away from priests' rights and personnel issues to the concerns of spritual and social ministries.

This policy has continued, under the leadership of Presidents Mayo and Ratigan, to the present time. The motif has been 'Serving the Ministering Church'. Convention themes and agendas for action have highlighted different dimensions of this theme. At Detroit in 1973, the focus was 'Pastoral Accountability'. At St. Petersburg, the theme was 'Reconciliation: Risks and Possibilities'. Last year at

Houston, it was 'Serving the Ministering Church'. This theme will be continued at the Louisville convention, 1977, which celebrates its tenth anniversary.

The federation has been at the cutting edge of the significant ecclesial and societal issues over the past decade. It provided a forum where all segments of society within and without the Church were heard and debated.

But the federation has never had the organizational resources and adequate structures to be truly effective with the rank and file priests. It has never been representative of the local clergy. Despite these defects, and for whatever reasons which produced them, the federation has opened the doors of archbishops and associate pastors alike. A policy, together with a variety of programs, has been institutionalized to insure that the opportunity for dialogue is ever present. Priests have the right to voice their ideas and concerns, their hurts and experiences. The NFPC is the only forum left for parish priests which provides the opportunity for such participation.

In launching well-nurtured activities into separate national organizations, such as continuing education, the rural ministry program, personnel administration, etc., the NFPC has kept its organization slim. This has allowed it to concentrate on its role of reconciler and facilitator, sharing and exchanging the ponderings of ministries of other priests and people.

The dialogues with the pastoral ministries have been on reconciling the issues of pro life, divorced Catholics, resigned priests, alienated youth, and ideological cleavages. The concerns of the social ministry have focused on racial inequality, women's rights, justice for the poor, world hunger, and corporate responsibility among others.

A great deal of the federation's activity as facilitator in the ministering church culminated in an event unique in U.S. Catholic history. It was an event in which members of the NFPC, past and present, at various levels, participated with religious and lay groups in a two year process which led to the 'Bicentennial Conference on Liberty and Justice for All'. The conference, however, was convened by the United States Catholic bishops, and this is what made the event significant.

The 'Call to Action' conference held in October of 1976 voiced demands which startled many bishops, especially since the NCCB hailed the conference as the most representative meeting in U.S. Catholic history. Furthermore, over 1100 of the 1340 official delegates were approved by their bishops.

And what were the demands of the people of God? They wanted changes. They wanted ordination of women, married priests, remarried divorced Catholics to be received back into the church, the norms of birth control to be determined by individual conscience, civil rights for homosexuals, establishment of a National Review Board to promote accountability at all levels of church government, broader participation in the selection of bishops, and to transform diocesan councils to policy making bodies. These resolutions coming from a broad representation of the Church reminds one of similar resolutions passed by the NFPC a decade ago. In the pages of this book, I call this first set of demands 'interest' issues dealing with the *rights* of God's people.

I also discuss in these pages another set of NFPC resolutions which are described as 'value' issues of the commonweal. The NCCB's Bicentennial Conference also addressed itself to these issues of social justice: racial equality, family stability, respect for ethnicity, disarmament, sexual equality, poverty and hunger, and other concerns of the social and pastoral ministry. These latter issues, as mentioned above, have been NFPC's primary agenda over the past five years. Although an interesting question might be how much influence the NFPC has had on this conference and its preparation, it is not as relevant as the question of what lies ahead for the future.

The NFPC has retooled and realigned its national committees and their responsibilities this past year. But whether the NFPC has the organizational resources and effective networks of communication, and whether its grassroots support, morale and commitment to the federation is strong enough to engage and challenge the NCCB to implement the resolutions adopted by their people are salient questions.

Answers, solutions, implementations, will be hard to come by regardless of any type and intensity of activity and even conflict. The NCCB is a non-binding structure with a greater part of its membership unable to fit participatory democracy into their ecclesiology.

Sociologically and theologically, it doesn't have the capability to implement. Its strength, in holding the line on change, lies in its organizational weakness. If, however, these matters are placed in a different context, then perhaps there is room for movement.

If this Detroit conference is viewed as providing directions, offering an opportunity to dialogue, and a process of accommodation in give and take exchanges, then the challenge and opportunity remain.

Which direction the federation will take is not answered in this book. This essay is mainly about its development over the past ten years, its mistakes and victories, its organizational development and vulnerability, its leadership and an uneven membership. It is about a cadre of brave priests and the rank and file of priests uninterested in the NFPC. In short, it is about a decade of turmoil.

In March, 1977, the NFPC celebrated its tenth birthday. As it moves into its second decade, will it take up again in significant ways the 'interest' issues mentioned above? Or will the federation continue to emphasize the value issues found in the pastoral and social ministry? Those answers are not to be found here. One may find, however, in this historical and sociological analysis of the past ten years, some clues which may help the NFPC to adequately prepare itself to decide which option it will emphasize and what policies it will pursue.

Ten years ago, democracy came knocking at the door of the Church. The NFPC let it in and the total Church hasn't been the same ever since. The 1968 delegates heard the militant voice of Joe O'Donaghue calling for massive involvement in the peace movement. The 1974 delegates heard the quiet voice of Cesar Chavez asking for the NFPC's support. Last year, they heard the Apostolic Delegate, Archbishop Jardot's brotherly exhortation to unity which is born from the exchanges of diverse views. If nothing else, the NFPC has provided priests with a forum to debate, a democracy, a voice. This option is precious. So whatever direction the federation decides to move, I wish it well on this tenth anniversary for it is a reason to hope.

April, 1977   JAMES H. STEWART

Contents

List of Tables and Figures

Troubled Transition in the Church

THE PRIESTHOOD AND THE COUNCIL'S DOCUMENTS

In their deliberations at Vatican II, the bishops of the world emphasized the roles of prelates and parishioners, and especially the poor of the world. With prelates the issue was authority and collegiality. Supreme power over the Church belongs to the bishops in union with the Pope. The expanded role of the laity emphasized their priesthood and their right to participate actively in the same service of God. The laity also possesses charisms, and it is the responsibility of the bishops to listen to and take advice from them. The Church Fathers also paid a great deal of attention to ecumenical relations with the rest of the Christian and non-Christian world. But what about the priesthood?

At the beginning of the Council, very little was said on the priesthood in the major documents. Because it was inadequately treated in the Constitution of the Church (*Lumen Gentium*), several separate drafts were prepared for the Third and Fourth Sessions, but it wasn't until late in the final session that a decree on the priesthood was passed (Abbott and Gallagher, 1966). One has only to read the tables of contents of books on Vatican II, such as Küng (1967), MacEoin (1966), and Novak (1964), to appreciate this lack of emphasis on the priesthood at the Council.

Many priests and especially some *periti* at the Council were quite disturbed with this turn of events. An unintended consequence of this less than thorough examination of the modern priesthood was the creation of further ambiguity in the definition of the priest. The decree on the priesthood emphasized the traditional definition of the priest as mediator between God and man through the Eucharist. It saw the priest as a delegate of the bishop and his power as an extension of the hierarchy. But nothing substantial was spelled out on the theological and structural meanings of collegiality as applied to the clergy. Still less was anything mentioned about the rights and freedoms of the priest. It seemed that the Council left the priests as marginal men between the bishop of whom they were an extension and the laity who they were to train as leaders of the community.

The Loss of Functions

This definition of the status of the priesthood came at a time when the priest in the United States was experiencing a loss of functions. With the rapid development of industrial technology, science, the professions, and other forms of knowledge, and the rapid increase of urbanization, the priest could no longer be, if he ever was, all things to all men (O'Dea, 1968: 21–24). Ministry was more purposeful when the immigrant population came to him for help, advice, and decisions. The priest fulfilled the expressive function of 'Father'. He served his flock, but he also ruled. His prestige came from two directions—love and respect. He combined quite nicely the expressive and instrumental roles of his office. The priesthood was defined theologically and legally for him, but he was able to work out that definition pragmatically to the fulfillment of his psychological and social needs.

But this was no longer possible. It became difficult for the priest to be 'Father' when he was serving large congregations. His people did not come to him for a wide range of advice. Instead, they went to professionals who had specialized knowledge and experience. Even in regard to certain theological and ethical questions many priests found themselves lost. Thus a dilemma arose for the priest. He was losing his functions. He was neither fully 'Father' nor fully a professional (Donovan, 1966: 113–120).

The problems of identity and self-worth are related to this structural dilemma. It is the dilemma of the priestly office seeking legitimacy in a bureaucratic society which values utilitarian function rather than the expressive activity of forming a community of faith. It is a society that rewards specialization and professionalism. The priest in the secular world is looked upon as a 'good guy' but is ignored or devalued because his credentials are not relevant.

The theology of the priesthood didn't provide answers to these dilemmas and questions. What is the proper ministry of the priest?

What can't a lay person do that a priest can do, except offer Mass and hear confessions? Is the secular world the sole domain of the priesthood of the laity? There was a crisis of the priesthood.

Before the Council, the priest lived in an atmosphere that stifled most questions or doubts he might have. Authority of the bishop and pastors has become so exalted and absolute that the priest, by and large, resigned himself to silence whenever he encountered irrelevant or harmful requirements. He helped count the Sunday collection because it was a good administrative experience. He obeyed his pastor and didn't go visiting the homes of the parishioners. He remained aloof from the people, remembering that his seminary training told him that a priest was set apart; but he also knew that the pastor was jealous of popular young priests. The priest was trained in obedience and docility to the point that he accepted infringements on, and injustices to, his personal rights as temptations of pride. Although this is an over-statement, it does characterize the climate in which a great number of priests lived and worked.

This climate of the church was depicted by Bernard M. Kelley, the Auxiliary Bishop of Providence, Rhode Island, in his letter of resignation (Cogley, 1973: 129):

.... The Vatican Council promised to bring the Church into the world but .... I have come to the painful conclusion that the United States Bishops ... are determined to preserve as far as possible the structure and forms of Trent.... I feel obliged in conscience to protest ... by my resignation.

PROBLEM OF DEFINITION

The crisis in the priesthood was indeed one of authority and leadership, and I will discuss this later. But central to the problem of the priesthood was the question of identification. What is the role of the priest? Just what can he do? There were lay leaders that told priests to stay out of the secular world. Ed Marciniak, a well-known social-actionist, attacked clerical activism as an encroachment on the role of the layman who is the secular 'insider', the initiate of an expertise quite different from the clergyman's. If conscience is going to mediate between moral teaching and politics while preserving the wall of separation between Church and State, then laymen must be the mediators. The clergy speak too directly of moral imperatives, making churchly claims too little negotiable, too unyielding, for the pluralistic marketplace (Wills, 1972: 151).

Marciniak has isolated the core issue of the definitional problem of the priesthood. Priests don't have the expertise—so stay out of society. From the passing of the *Gemeinschaft* society to the *Gesellschaft* society, the principle of competence has replaced the principle of investiture; specialization has ruled out the notion of universal competence. No one any longer sees the 'power of orders' as the source of all types of diversified expertise in the Church or in society. Such expertise assumes a long period of special training and long practical experience (Pin, 1969: 53).

That is why many priests, especially the younger ones, felt inadequate for the tasks that they were assigned. They felt ill-trained in counselling and human relations skills, as well as lacking in personal growth and maturity (Kennedy and Heckler, 1971: 7–13). They pointed to the inadequacy of their seminary training. Fichter (1968: 204–205), in a study of American priests who were not pastors, states that these respondents reported a deficient career preparation for the very functions that absorb most of their time and energy. They were constantly dealing with people, counselling them, serving them, and yet they complained that they had practically no training in social relations or in how to handle practical organizational problems.

The basic fault did not lie with the seminary but with the Church leadership in not apprising themselves of the changing needs of society and of the trends calling for new professional values. The priestly role and definition didn't mesh well with the reality of modern society, and this lack of articulation between what a priest was trained to do and the requirements of the pastoral and social ministry has caused the crisis of definition and identity (see Stewart, 1969a).

As mentioned, the Council didn't clarify matters either. In the document *Presbyterorum Ordinis,* the Council explicitly affirmed the need for order and structure, emphasizing the importance of priestly collaboration with the bishops in sanctifying and governing the

Church. Priests were viewed as 'prudent cooperators' with the episcopal order and its aids and instruments. Yet, on the other hand, the bishops stated that 'all the faithful of Christ of whatever rank and status are called to the fullness of Christian life and to the perfection of charity'. And in pursuing that common vocation, 'Christians cannot yearn for anything more ardently than to serve the men of the modern world ever more generously and effectively'. The Council held out a new but confused vision of the priesthood that contrasted sharply with the actual life of the diocesan priest (O'Brien, 1971: 452).

But this new vision became painful to many priests when they reflected on their professional inadequacies. Experiencing both frustration and anger, many became rebellious and confrontative (see Ellis, 1969: 163–255). O'Brien (1971: 452) expressed the dilemma in this way:

> Caught in the conflict of loyalties to the institutional forms in which he has been trained and through which he had worked, and his equally powerful desire for thorough professional training and for the freedom to identify with the cause of the poor ... the priest necessarily entered a period of anxiety and unrest.

The Council told all Christians to exercise their freedom and use their judgment in renewing the ministry of Christ in the modern world. Priests, religious, and laity alike took the advice seriously. The questioning and open discussion began, sometimes logically and responsibly, sometimes not. But the discussions did make priests aware of their common problems. However, their reactions were not all the same.

A large number of priests went calmly about their ritual functions as if the Council had hardly happened. Some were annoyed because the Council called for a change in the routines. These tended to be older priests who had worked out a model of separating the sacred and profane. Their only concerns were to preserve the style of the ministry to which they were accustomed and to hold onto certain interests that they had gained.

A second group of priests, mostly younger men, was unable to reconcile this new vision of the Council and the institutionalized routines of pastoral work. Obedience and celibacy, in particular, became intolerable constraints. The Council had emphasized obedient submissiveness over personal responsibility. Moreover, theology was rediscovering the spiritual significance of sexual relationships (Pin, 1969: 50). This had an impact on the thinking of many priests. For these men, authority was repressive and the institution of the priesthood was no fraternity, but a lonely crowd. Many began to resign from the ministry.

A third group experienced a deep insecurity. They were neither young nor old. They had worked very hard in their parishes, especially in building and expanding Catholic schools. Many were the post-war, brick-and-mortar priests, but much of what they did was peripheral to the pastoral ministry itself. Time was consumed with administration and management (Roche, 1968: 182). They were priests who, on the whole, would not be leaders of renewal. They waited for leadership to develop, expecting it to come from the bishop. They became confused and sometimes angry at younger priests for taking initiative and leadership.

The last group sought to implement the new goals of the post-conciliar Church in whatever ways possible. These priests were in their 30s and 40s. Though they were troubled and frustrated at the pace of renewal in the diocese, they didn't have the insecurities or needs of the other three groups. They weren't concerned with the symbols and prerogatives of status. These men had the conviction that they had a share in making the renewal work. Most also had the courage and perseverance to 'hand in'. Garry Wills (1972: 246) captured the sentiment of some of this group in the following statement:

> Those Catholics who go underground would not be so offensive to 'normal' Catholics if it meant going out—leaving the Church, the priesthood, the Christian fellowship, once and for all. Timorous episcopal 'fishers of men' would gladly shake these fish out of their nets; but the unwanted catch just laughs and hangs in there. Philip writes to Daniel, 'We'll muckle through for old Mother Church'. Daniel says that the institutional Church nibbled away at Christ. Yet Christ was there to be nibbled at .... Mother [Church] may be a wacky dame at best, but these disturbing sons ... pay her the compliment of finding her 'serious' and 'interesting'.

These priests saw the Church as a servant of mankind. For them the incarnation of Christ continued in His people, giving hope and seeking justice for all mankind. They weren't content with a narrow definition of the ministry. They were 'value'-oriented, concerned about the needs and rights of the common weal. They weren't taken by clerical interests, prerogatives, and status. But they were very concerned that their world-view would have little meaning and relevance without experience and competencies.

THE MALAISE

These years immediately following the Council were times, then, of theological controversy, discontent, turmoil, and great discouragement. It was a stormy period when laity were increasingly ignoring Church law about such things as Mass attendance and birth control regulations. Priests were resigning in great numbers. Seminaries were closing. It seemed for a time that the Church was experiencing wholesale anomie and facing widespread disintegration. The whole edifice of law, custom, and religious practice that had supported Catholic stability since the Council of Trent was threatened (Cogley, 1973: 125–26).

Whether it was the bishops who were primarily to blame for the crisis of American Catholics, particularly the priests, or whether it was the impatience of priests and laity who pressed for changes beyond Vatican II, is not the relevant question here. What is important is the nature and consequences of an irrelevant definition of the priesthood. A solution to this crisis would go far in solving other problems related to this definitional one. The problems of authority, leadership, and freedom; of institutionalization and personal autonomy; and of faith and a meaningful world-view are directly tied to the crisis of identity (see Greeley, 1972a).

Many priests were troubled because they were continually frustrated by the institutional rigidity of the Church. They found themselves helpless and powerless. They were torn between loyalty to the Church organization and their commitments to the needs of the people. They saw the Church as a total institution allowing little freedom to experiment. Many also found themselves harassed or punished if they entered social controversies. For some the Church became an obstacle to faith in the ministry of serving the societal needs. For others the Church ceased to be an authentic sign of Christ. Priests saw many of their leaders living comfortably, with little concern about matters of social justice. Frequently enough they incurred their bishops' displeasure for being involved. Thus arose the problem of disbelief in the Church as a meaningful sign of salvation. This problem became more acute because the blanket of legitimacy over episcopal authority had been thrown off. Many priests no longer believed in their bishops, nor in the priesthood.

THE FRATERNITY

Priests also had problems with one another. They experienced difficulty in cooperating with each other. Moreover, the clerical caste system didn't evidence a sense of fraternity and mutual support. Related to this was the problem of episcopal distance. The bishop wasn't viewed as an elder brother in the presbytery but, often as not, as a man removed and feared. There was neither redress of grievances nor mechanisms for control of the arbitrary use of authority. Collegiality was yet to be born (see Greeley, 1967; Commonweal, 1968a and 1968b).

Without this fraternity and support, priests experienced loneliness and isolation. They had the ordinary needs of human persons for companionship, compassion, and understanding. For many the priesthood itself didn't satisfy these needs. Moreover, Church policy discouraged them from mixing with the laity for fear that priests become a source of rumor and gossip. Many adjusted reasonably well to this situation. Some simply resigned. Others who didn't resign developed problems with alcohol and mental illness. Others frittered away empty days with poker and the horse races to keep their sanity. Thus the priesthood faced a general malaise in the post-council period which shook its very foundation. I will now turn to some specifics.

AUTHORITY AND AUTONOMY

Every organization needs authority to set goals and coordinate activities. The Church is no exception. Hence it is not a question of authority, but of how authority is to be structured and exercised. Modern organizations are essentially interdependent systems based on the need of mutual competencies and specializations. Because knowledge is so vast and specialized, authority must be shared and coordinated. The pluralistic and decentralized nature of modern bureaucracies requires broad participation in decision making. The function of authority is to promote the most intelligent kind of participation (Greeley, 1966: 61–70).

Effective decision making, then, rests on study, discussion, and expertise. The decisions in a specific area are left to those who are more knowledgeable. This autonomy builds morale and increases motivation. Application of these principles to the ministry would help it to be more effective because there would be a greater respect for personal and professional freedom and little waste of talent. This type of authority would satisfy important psychological needs of freedom, creativity, and growth (see Kennedy and Heckler, 1971; Hall and Schneider, 1973). The Council understood the implications of modernity. It saw the need for subsidiarity and autonomy, on the one hand, and collegiality and shared responsibility on the other. But these ideas were not clearly spelled out in terms of bishop-priests relationships on the local diocesan level.

Back in the home dioceses there was control and silencing of those priests pressing for decentralization, arguing for autonomy of thought and action, and seeking social change. This suppression was demonstrated by the words of Father Peter Riga, a nationally known student of the Church's social teachings (Roche, 1968: 183):

When you get home from a chancery office after being told that you may not speak on Vietnam when your conscience tells you to speak, or that your sermons 'disturb' people because you tell them of their sins of racism and heartlessness with regard to the poor—then you go to your lonely room and cry. . . .

In his study of American priests, Fichter (1968: 203–04) found that the basic expectation of the priests was that authority required wide consultation, free and open two-way communication, a willingness by superiors to credit them with maturity, and an honest admission that neither their decisions nor the implementation of them can be the work of one man alone. But in reality, many priests who first tried to take seriously the Council declaration that every Christian had to make his own responsible judgments and act accordingly were both undercut and sanctioned by their superiors.

Priests began to define the people of God as something larger than the Church. They assumed para-relationships with the bishop and chancery office. This often neutralized the bishop's power without creating any confrontation. Such ignoring of authority was probably a more lethal weapon in the erosion of episcopal power than anything else. Osborne states (1969: 47):

> Chancery directives and policy they douse with salt and mix with their own common sense and conscience. The norm of obedience is thus being transformed into one which allows for authority, yet brings into play humane and religious values prior to ecclesiastical goals and values.

Matters went even further. More and more priests no longer felt bound by everything the Pope and bishops decreed. Many did not accept the official teaching of the Church on birth control, celibacy, and divorce. Married priests were performing the liturgy in underground churches; others were telling parishioners that it was all right to use artificial contraceptives, and some were performing marriages among divorced Catholics. Furthermore, some began publicly to announce their dissent. For instance, a group of priests in the Washington, D.C., Archdiocese caused national headlines by stating that the issue of birth control should be left up to the individual conscience. Some were suspended by Cardinal O'Boyle without due process. Their case was finally settled after a three-year ordeal.

What was happening to priests was that a basic change of perspective toward authority was taking place. Blind acceptance of ecclesiastical documents and episcopal decisions would no longer happen. The Pope and the bishops would have to provide rationales to convince their people of the wisdom and rightness of their statements (Cogley, 1973: 123).

THE LEADERSHIP VACUUM

As painful as the authority crisis was, a more crucial problem was the lack of leadership. Prior to the Council, most of the episcopal leaders were legal and managerial types. Higher degrees among the bishops were most likely to be either licentiates in theology from the North American College in Rome or doctorates in canon law. The bishops did not have reputations as theologians or scholars of the arts and sciences. They were not the leaders of the liturgy and social justice.

One did not find in the pre-Council hierarchy men like Murray, Weigel, Ellis, Hellriegel, Hillenbrand, LaFarge, Higgens, Egan, Putz, and Gremillon. It was the influence of such men that was to be the source of leadership, filling in the vacuum of the late 1960s. Within the framework of the Church they knew, the bishops limited their leadership to building up the immigrant Church spiritually, educationally, and, not least of all, physically.

When the Council came, the bishops depended a great deal on their *periti*. In attending one session of the Council, I was surprised to find that the bishops were taking, on the side, brush-up courses in theology and scripture from the renowned *periti* of the Council. The point is that the bishops went home insecure and bewildered with what they had wrought. They were especially fearful that power would slip from their hands, not because of a loss of personal prestige, but because diocesan power had traditionally been defined in their office. Some thought that it would be immoral, if not heretical, to share this power.

More importantly, the bishops didn't know how to lead or innovate. They were used to a leadership which stabilized and managed spiritual and temporal affairs. It was anathema for them to make mistakes, especially ecclesiastical ones. Overwhelmed with responsibility and inexperienced at innovation, they waited for Rome to act.

Most of the bishops, then, were unequipped to develop replacement models for developing norms and values that were relevant and meaningful for their people. They were unable to engender a sense of purpose, wonder, and even excitement about the renewal of the gospel. They were not wise men providing steady but forward steps through the turmoils of uncertainty.

TOTAL INSTITUTION

Besides the leadership crisis there was the problem of institutionalization. The impersonal processes of the large-scale diocese submerged the personal life of the priest. The fact that the rectory office was also his home symbolized that the priest had gone public, but with much bitterness and alienation on his part. He had no life of his own. The artificial and sometimes oppressive relationships in the rectory turned him into a lonely man. If he was an innovator, the fraternity would peg him as an oddball.

CRISIS OF FAITH

This period was a time of questioning just about everything in the Church. The bishops were learning painfully to consult with their priests. Nuns were no longer hidden in the convents. Lay leaders demanded to be heard. The one, holy, catholic, and apostolic Church was in the throes of a democratic revolution. According to a Harris poll taken at this time (*Newsweek*, 1967), 70% of the laity wanted the Church to lift its ban on birth control. About 60% would approve abortion if the life of the mother was at stake, and about 65% said they would like to see the Pope provide annulments allowing the remarriage of the innocent party. These findings suggest that American Catholics were moving away from the moral standards regarding family life as taught by the hierarchy.

Moreover, the younger and better-educated laity, as well as many priests, were aware that the mind of the Church on fundamental questions of faith was no longer made of whole cloth. Theologians lined up on both sides of a question. For instance, Gregory Baum (*Newsweek*, 1967) argued that as man changes so does his perception of truth, such as in the doctrine of infallibility. He thought that this doctrine needed reformulation in the light of modern culture. But other theologians and Pope Paul himself condemned the relativistic mentality that destroys objective truth. Many Catholic scholars believed that the mysteries of faith cannot be interpreted by the Church from one philosophical framework. And so confusion and debate continued.

SOLUTIONS TO ANOMIE

The Council held out a new vision of man and the world. New expectations and goals were set forth, but the norms and means of implementation were lacking. The expressive goals of the Church require communities in which members are regarded as persons rather than as employees, and this is a major dilemma of the contemporary Catholic Church. With a highly centralized structure, the Church must confront demands for new services and innovations arising from Vatican II, as well as from pressures arising from the secular world with its need for competencies. The bishops are faced with the alternative of allowing greater voice to those who possibly do not share their own outlook or of losing the loyalty of many of their 'employees', the priests.

In the meantime, priests on their own have begun to take steps to attain these goals of renewal. The motivation for this activity was certainly due to the Vatican Council, but the rapid changes in the secular milieu also accounted for these aspirations.

Priests were seeking the attainment of such human values as (1) recognition and respect from their bishops; (2) confidence in the knowledge that what they are doing is worthwhile and meaningful to them and to those they serve; (3) a feeling of belonging and acceptance among their fellow priests, regardless of their work and outlook; (4) a sense of freedom and responsible autonomy to experiment in applying the expectations of Vatican II to their local situations without fear of punishment; (5) the importance of redirecting priestly activities to the crucial needs of the poor and oppressed; (6) professional rights and due process to protect their work and good name from ill-formed or misguided sanctions; and (7) privacy of life and optional celibacy (Fichter, 1968).

These men were faced with the problems of adjustments both in their ministerial roles and in their personal lives. They sought solutions to both the structural problems in which there were few articulated responses for renewing the pastoral mission and to the personal meaninglessness of the priesthood. But how to begin? From where would the leadership come?

Priest-leaders in the lay, social action, and civil rights apostolates began to interact and to communicate with one another, seeking opportunities for advice and direction on how to proceed with renewal. A historical landmark was a meeting in Chicago of priests from all over the country. They came as observers to the second congress of the Association of Chicago Priests in the spring of 1967. Through subsequent meetings of a similar nature, there was created 'The National Federation of Priests' Councils' (NFPC) in May, 1968.

At about the same time, several other priests' organizations were formed, including 'The National Association for Pastoral Renewal' (NAPR) and 'The Society of Priests for the Free Ministry' (SPFM). These organizations represented the 'left-wing' of the Church.

Two other groups were formed in reaction to the changes that had taken place already, especially in the area of liturgy and religious education. One was called 'The Catholic Traditionist Movement' (CTM); the other was 'Catholics United for the Faith' (CUF). All five of these organizations evolved without the membership seeking approval for their existence and activities from the bishops.

A TYPOLOGY OF ORGANIZATIONAL RESPONSES TO ANOMIC CONDITIONS

The organizational responses of the NFPC, NAPR, SPFM, CUF, and the CTM provided different opportunities for priests and laity relative to the anomic conditions found in Catholicism shortly after Vatican II. The NFPC provided access to unconventional means in attaining the goals of a relevant ministry. While abiding by the norm of celibacy, the members were mobilizing their talents and energies for renewal through unauthorized means. In short, their earlier tactics were to institutionalize innovation and militancy *vis-à-vis* the bishops.

The NAPR and SPFM also accepted the goal of a renewed priesthood, but many of its members rejected the norm of celibacy. Thus, the membership of the NAPR was composed of a significant number of priests who had resigned, many of whom had also married. During this time, some had set up alternative forms of the ministry and continued to offer the liturgy, usually with 'underground churches'. They represent a form of rebellion.

Table 1.1   *A typology of organizational responses to anomie*

Mode of adaptation	Organizational response	Orthodox means	Cultural goals of renewed priesthood
Conformity	NCCB (and Senates)	+	+
Innovation	NFPC	–	+
Ritualism	—	+	–
Retreatism	CTM, CUF	–	–
Rebellion	SPFM, NAPR	±	±

The members of CTM were retreatists who rejected the goal of renewal and the legitimate means of modernizing the priesthood. They were traditionalists who clung to the Latin liturgy and rigorously conformed to priestly conduct based on outdated norms.

The CUF members were also retreatist. They wanted to preserve Catholic doctrine in the form and substance of the Baltimore Catechism.

Finally, the NCCB (the organization of bishops) and, on the local scene, most diocesan senates, represented the conformists' response. Adaptation to change would take place in an orderly way guided by ecclesiastical authority.

The means-end model of Merton's deviant adaptations to anomie provides a typology of organizational responses to the structural strain felt by a sizeable number of priests, as presented in Table 1.1. (See Merton, 1957: 131–94.)

THE NATIONAL FEDERATION OF PRIESTS' COUNCILS

Where will the Church find its leaders? This book is about one source of leadership. The NFPC has taken up the challenge of renewal. In the process, it has moved away from what Allport calls extrinsic religion, with its fixed dogmas and norms, toward an intrinsic religion, based on the inspiration of the gospel and the human condition. How well the NFPC is doing the job of service is another question. This book is primarily a sociological analysis of its effectiveness. It interprets the NFPC's worth from its foundation to 1975.

The NFPC has been an ongoing attempt to provide leadership, relevancy, and models for the pastoral and social ministry. In a period when the Church was losing five priests through death, retirement, or resignation for every two seminarians it ordained (*Newsweek*, 1971b), the NFPC became a mechanism to bargain with the bishops. At times there was eyeball-to-eyeball confrontation, but most often the NFPC initiated strategies, sometimes quite subtly, to bring democracy, autonomy, and professionalism to the ranks of the clergy.

Some senates might deny that the NFPC has any influence in the diocese, but one wonders where local councils would be without this national organization. It has taken on tough issues, such as due process and professional rights. It has been very effective on these and other issues, such as social justice programs.

The NFPC was responsible for the establishment of the National Association of Church Personnel Administrators, the National Organization for Continuing Education of Roman Catholic Clergy, and the National Catholic Coalition for Responsible Investment. It efforts have been with the farm workers, peace education, amnesty, and religious education.

The NFPC has muddled through some issues and has made mistakes in policy and organizational development, but it is a sign of courage, leadership, and vision. Most readers will remember the state of turmoil and paralysis, the frustration and depression, that the Church experienced in 1967 and 1968. The NFPC was born out of this situation. Priests were hurting. The hierarchy was in a quandary. But there were priests of vision and courage who would design and create a representative organization. It would be an organization set up in an autonomous and democratic way. However, this was organizational deviance par excellence, for nothing touching the priesthood has ever existed in the American Church without hierarchial approval. But exist it does, as a representative voice of priests calling for a more realistic participation in the Church's decision making.

An important goal of the NFPC is to clarify and redefine the role of the priest, still one of the major problems facing the priesthood. Utilizing the wisdom and experience of local councils, the NFPC is steadily reshaping this definition of the priest. It has the capacity to do this because policies, goals, and models of the ministry come from the grassroots. Democracy is an arduous process within the priesthood, but it has given dignity and power to those who were an afterthought of the Council.

Although at times it has been difficult, the NFPC has combined within itself two structural and ideological variations, the senates and free associations. This duality has provided the NFPC with both flexibility and creativity, on the one hand, and a balance and stability on the other. With these ingredients built into the structure of the NFPC, the priesthood of the United States has a reason for hope. I will now turn to discuss how the NFPC was launched.

2

Beginnings of the Federation

The Vatican Council called for impossible things. Pope John XXIII issued a mandate for renewal and change. Along with this mandate, Pope Paul VI called for unity and peace. But, within a few years, turmoil replaced peace and a division between traditionalists and progressives fractured the unity of the Roman Catholic Church.

Modernization of the Church called for the abolishment of authoritarianism and institutionalized legalisms. The frustration and discontent with the pace of renewal was primarily felt by the middle leadership of the Church. It was priests and religious who were at the forefront of rebellion. Documents of Vatican II, such as *Christus Dominus* and *Presbyterorum Ordinis*, held out high, but confusing, expectations for renewing the ministry and life of the clergy. The failure of ecclesiastical leadership not only to implement the documents' recommendations with due speed, but also to develop a replacement theory for interpreting modern Christianity and the priesthood, increased the clergy's sense of bewilderment and powerlessness. Yet priest leaders kept hoping and pressing for a new relevancy. This paradox of disillusionment and hope was chronicled by a Catholic journalist who provides us with the following impressions:

> Everywhere I traveled I found people either disappointed or unimpressed with the bishops as leaders.... Against this crisis of authority must be balanced the new creativity working its way into the life of the Church. What I see as a creative revolution is the second major impression of my travels (Roche, 1968: xxi-xxii).

This problem hasn't gone away. Greeley (1972a: 9–10) found that the most serious problem still facing priests was that of authority. It wasn't that authority was as oppressive in 1972 as it once had been, but that the problem became one of a collapse of credibility and consensus.

VATICAN II AND PRIESTS' COUNCILS

In the eyes of many then, the hope of renewing the priesthood and ministry rested not with episcopal leadership but with the clergy itself. The Vatican II recommendations on priests' councils facilitated the efforts of priests to take hold of this responsibility. The Decree *Christus Dominus*, proclaimed by Pope Paul VI on October 28, 1965 (Abbott and Gallagher, 1966: 416), states:

Included among the collaborators of the bishop in the government of the diocese are those priests who constitute his senate or council, such as the cathedral chapter, the board of consultors, or other committees established according to the circumstances or nature of various localities. To the extent necessary, these institutions, especially the cathedral chapters, should be reorganized in keeping with present-day needs.

Priests and lay people who belong to the diocesan curia should realize that they are making a helpful contribution to the pastoral ministry of the bishop.

The diocesan curia should be so organized that it is an appropriate instrument for the bishop, not only for administering the diocese but also for carrying out the works of the apostolate.

This new concept of clergy consultation and representation was further specified by the *Motu Proprio* letter of Pope Paul VI (1966: 15) entitled *Ecclesiae Sanctae:*

(1) In each diocese, according to a method and plan to be determined by the bishop, there should be a council of priests, that is a group or senate of priests who represent the body of priests and who by their counsel can effectively assist the bishop in the government of the diocese. In this council the bishop should listen to his priests, consult them and have dialogue with them on those matters which pertain to the needs of pastoral work and the good of the diocese.

(2) Religious may also be named members of the council of priests to the extent that they have the care of souls and take part in the works of the apostolate.

(3) The council of priests has only a consultative vote.

(4) When the See becomes vacant, the council of priests ceases unless in special circumstances to be reviewed by the Holy See the

vicar capitular or apsotolic administrator confirms its existence. The new bishop will establish his own new council of priests.

The first council or senate was established in Springfield, Massachusetts, on January 20, 1966 (Kennedy, 1968: 167–68). By May, 1968, there were 135 senates and 28 free associations in operation. These two council types do not have a lot in common. Senates (1) are authorized in the dioceses by the bishops and serve at their pleasure; (2) exist to assist the bishop in the area of the priestly role, diocesan government, personnel policy, organizational problems of the diocese, and pastoral matters; (3) have an approach which is primarily cooperative; (4) are advisory; (5) are conforming organizations considered legitimate by the bishop (see Stewart, 1970; Wuerl, 1970).

The free associations, on the other hand, (1) were established without the authorization or subsequent approval of their bishops; (2) work more independently of the bishops but, at the same time, submit programs of action to them and work for their acceptance. The proposals center around the values of the priest's person; of his rights; and of the pastoral mission as it relates to the issues of equality, freedom, and justice. Some associations have set up 'watch dog' committees to protect priests from unjust sanctions. The association's approach (3) is more combative; it is willing to use public media to make its position clear. The basic operational policy is to raise questions and press the bishop to face certain issues. The associations (4) have no legitimate power. In sum, the associations are deviant organizations and lack legitimacy as far as the bishops are concerned (see Stewart, 1970).

Further guidelines for establishing priests' councils were formulated by the Congregation for the Clergy in October, 1969 (Wright, 1970: 53–57). While these guidelines describe the nature, responsibilities, and general purposes of priests' councils, they stress that councils do not have a deliberative role, except in individual cases designated by the bishop. Furthermore, the guidelines state that, based on the need for common pastoral activity in which the priests and bishop unite to make their work more effective, the council has a special consultative role in advising the bishop upon request. The council, according to the document, is to help, but not replace, the authority and work of the bishop.

Most priests were both confused about the actual structure and operation of these new councils and unhappy at the severe limitation of the power that the councils possessed. Many felt that the notion of authority relations between the bishop and the presbyterium was too narrowly defined within a legal framework. Many priests understood that Vatican II had called for a collegial sharing of authority. They saw authority as one charism which was present in the whole church and not only in the bishops. In the words of Padovano (1970: 207–08):

> The law of mutual dependence is a fundamental law governing the life of the Church. It justifies the principles of decentralization, subsidiarity, co-responsibility, and collegiality.

Padovano went on to state that senates as representative bodies should not be merely consultative but possess pastoral, charismatic, and sacramental authority which is inherent in the presbyterium and not delegated from the bishop.

The ministry as a function of shared authority was part of a new theology that many priests embraced. Many bishops, however, viewed this as a threat to their office. Some refused to establish senates; other ignored the advice of their councils; still others disbanded councils. In sum, many bishops felt that, while the councils did not have legal authority to make decisions, they could exercise a rather strong moral influence. This they felt would be a threat to the office of the ordinary as presently defined.

Another problem priests faced was that they didn't know how to go about structuring a council which would not only be truly representative but also be democratic in its deliberations. Moreover, they didn't know what functions and activities should be included or what their relationships should be with diocesan consultors and with religious and lay organizations.

One experience which helped priests to formalize the structure of the senates was their work with parish organizations. Most parish organizations had some type of constitution and bylaws. Priests seized this mechanisms to begin defining the councils' purposes, structures, and tasks. Most of these diocesan councils constituted themselves independently of each other. At this early stage, there was no thought of inter-diocesan cooperation. The reason for this is probably due to the fact that they had little experience with inter-cooperation. Dioceses were independent areas of ministry. I will now discuss briefly these early constitutions.

In 1967, I did an analysis of 123 bylaws and constitutions of diocesan councils. There were: ninety-nine senates (80%), twenty-two associations (18%), and two religious order councils (2%). One noticeable difference between the structure of the senates and the associations is that all the associations elected their members, whereas a number of senates have both elected and appointed members. The constitutions and bylaws of a large minority of both senates and associations evidenced a lack of constitutional provisions and specifications of procedures (see Table 2.1 below). The reason for this, I suggest, is the newness of priests' councils.

The overwhelming majority of councils has advisory powers only. Their general purposes are to represent their fellow priests regarding diocesan issues and affairs and to communicate and advise their respective bishops concerning these matters. None of the councils are any more specific in stating their goals than to say that the council gives advice to the bishop and acts as an agent for a two-way

Table 2.1   *Profile of local councils' constitutions* $(N = 123)$

Formal structure	Respondents N	%
Purposes of Council re:		
Fellow priests:		
Representation and communication	117	95
No data	6	5
The bishop:		
Advice and communication	109	89
No data	14	11
Powers of the Council		
Advisory only	100	82
Legislative with veto by bishop	5	4
No data	18	14
Representatives		
0–9	17	14
10–19	44	36
20 and over	37	30
No data	25	20

Table 2.1   *Continued*

Formal structure	Respondents N	%
Method of selection		
Elected	105	85
Elected and appointed	14	12
No data	4	3
Have an Executive Board		
Yes	66	54
No	18	15
No data	39	31
Parliamentary rules employed		
Yes	86	70
No	2	2
No data	35	28
Channels of communication with bishop		
Yes	69	56
No	—	—
No data	54	44
Dues required		
Yes	29	24
No	25	20
No data	69	56
Powers of Committees		
Advisory	73	59
Policy	—	—
No data	50	41

flow of communication. Most of the councils are formally weak regarding the possession and use of legitimate power. It is problematic how much real, though informal, power each council possesses through its moral persuasion. It is important to note that, though the senates are constituted only with the permission of the bishops, a large number of them have allowed elections to determine the composition of the senates. The average number of committees that the councils have is five. Those committees most frequently cited in the documents are: (1) Election, (2) Communication, and (3) Pastoral Ministry. In summary, the councils are at this time muddling through their organizational development. There is neither past precedent nor a national clearinghouse to provide advice and experience for forming these units. Only with the founding of the NFPC did the councils begin to consolidate and develop specific directions.

The priests of the United States were not only concerned about the leadership vacuum of the hierarchy and the lack of shared responsibility; they were also concerned with the issues of personal freedom and rights. Priests felt that as human beings they should have the same right as any other person to exercise the freedom of speech and to protect one's reputation. They felt that they had to speak from their consciences and say disturbing things not only to their parishioners but also to their bishops. These and many more got into trouble with their bishops and were arbitrarily sanctioned. They protested that their rights and reputations were being violated. Yet there was no adequate procedure of due process to settle these grievances. Monsignor Conway (1966: 200) urged such mechanisms when he wrote:

> Whatever the machinery is it must be of such nature that the priest who believes himself unjustly treated can appeal without prejudice to his standing in the diocese. He must not be subject to recriminations for trying to vindicate his rights. Pope John told us that we have a duty to do this.

Another proposal to insure the protection of priests' rights came from a different direction. Father William DuBay proposed what amounted to a national labor union of priests. Many thought that this idea would create greater discord between bishops and priests and divisions between priests and laity. The plan never got off the ground (O'Gara, 1966: 72). During 1966 and 1967, individual priests like Fathers Peter Riga, Robert Francoeur, James Drane, Dan and Phil Berrigan, and James Groppi were among those voicing opposition. They made national news because of their controversial statements and actions.

Another organizational development critical of the bishops' leadership was the National Association for Pastoral Renewal. At its height it had a membership of 3,500 active and resigned priests.

Although the NAPR was interested in implementing many renewal programs, its primary interest was the issue of optional celibacy. Its most noteworthy activity was sponsoring a national symposium on celibacy at the University of Notre Dame during the summer of 1967. Also, through a series of surveys during this period of time, the NAPR discovered that about 48 % of the priests of the country favored optional celibacy. The American hierarchy responded to these findings by stating that 'it would be irresponsible on our part to hold out any hope that this discipline would change'.

For the most part, however, the responses calling for renewal and the criticisms of the hierarchy came from individual and isolated priests, religious, and laity.

As I have shown, priests' councils were still in a gestating stage. There was no coordination or unified thrust among them. Most were under the authority of the bishop. Would any national voice and action develop among priests in the United States? Where would such united efforts spring from?

BEGINNINGS OF COLLECTIVE ACTION

The Archdiocese of Chicago had a long tradition of bishops who allowed their priests to develop leadership in the areas of the liturgy, social and economic justice, and the lay apostolate. Men like Monsignors Hillenbrand, Cantwell, and Egan were nationally respected leaders. They brought new ideas and programs into the church. Hillenbrand expanded the lay apostolate by applying the *jocist* techniques to families, workers, and students. Cantwell involved the church in racial and economic issues. Egan committed the archdiocese to the community organization philosophy of Saul Alinsky.

Cardinal Meyer was a champion of religious liberty. His untimely death and the appointment of his successor, Archbishop Cody, a strong-willed authority figure, brought about a morale crisis among the Chicago clergy. Before Archbishop Cody officially arrived in Chicago, sixteen priests were meeting secretly to mobilize their colleagues to form an association of priests. The one who spearheaded this effort was Father John Hill, an associate to

Monsignor Egan at Presentation parish. After several public meetings, attended by several hundred priests, Hill and several other priests approached Archbishop Cody for recognition of the new association. After a number of tense meetings and negotiations, the Archbishop finally agreed to its creation.

The Association of Chicago Priests (ACP) was among the first of the independently formed councils of priests. It was democratically structured to represent all the priests' concerns to the Archbishop. It had a considerable degree of autonomy and influence compared to senates. It moved quickly into ministerial issues such as election of bishops and formation of parish lay councils. Its agenda also included the social justice ministry. Father Raymond Goedert said (Roche, 1968: 201):

> Our most important accomplishment has been the development of a professional organization independent of the chancery office and yet without excluding the bishop. This has been a creative act and the priests' morale has improved, especially by the kind of seminars we hold.

The ACP also sponsored symposia featuring such outstanding theologians as Küng, Schillebeeckx, Cooke, and Häring. These theologians of renewal attracted the attention of priests outside Chicago. Many of these priests were known to each other because of their involvements in the lay, liturgical, and social apostolates. In January and February, some of these men had begun informal discussions with the Chicago leaders about the possibility of some joint collaboration. On May 8, 1967, they attended, as observers, the second plenary session of the ACP. Through prior arrangements, they asked the Chicago leaders to set up an ad hoc meeting for discussing some type of national cooperation.

This meeting was held on May 9, 1967. Father William Graney spoke to eighty-eight eastern and midwestern priests about the need for mutual assistance on a national level. He stated that senates and associations of priests, in and of themselves, are no guarantee of the rights of priests. The discussions centered around a reporting of what was being done by the individual chapters, especially in terms of structural development and the feasibility of, and procedures for, establishing a national association.

Father John Daily moved to establish an ad hoc committee to

study the need for a national association and to contact the local senates and associations for their reactions. It would also act as a steering committee to convene meetings of the local councils. Father Robert Kennedy from Brooklyn was unanimously chosen as chairman of the committee. Father Graney of Chicago was selected as public relations officer. Father Bob Malm from Brooklyn was appointed treasurer. Father John Hill was asked to receive the names of other dioceses interested in a national association. Father Kennedy was given the responsibility of selecting the members of the steering committee (Minutes, 1967).

On May 31, there was a meeting of this committee in Philadelphia to interest priests from the East Coast in the idea of a national federation. Kennedy also called monthly liaison meetings throughout the summer between leaders from the East Coast and the Midwest. On June 20, Father Kennedy and a group of midwestern priests met in Chicago to discuss the feasibility of a regional meeting.

COMMITTEE OF EIGHT

On July 13, this group was expanded to what was to be known as the 'Committee of Eight'. It was decided to hold a regional meeting in September. The purpose was primarily to provide an informational exchange meeting regarding the problems and experiences of the councils in the Midwest. They felt that the idea of a national collaboration should not be emphasized at this September meeting. The agenda and details of the September meeting were formulated at a meeting on August 25.

The 'Committee of Eight', representing eight midwestern provinces, was responsible for contacting the councils in the forty-two dioceses and seeking their advice and participation in the formation of the September agenda. These leaders were a bit cautious at this time about promoting the idea of a national association for fear that they might be charged with forcing the notion on local councils. Also, they did not know what reactions to expect from the bishops. As will be shown shortly, there was no need for an alarm. At the same time that this meeting was being planned, Father Kennedy was planning a winter meeting of councils in the New England area.

On September 8, 1967, the following press release was issued by Father Graney:

A Midwest regional meeting on Catholic priests' councils will be held in Chicago on Sept. 25 and 26.

Priests from a 10-state area in the Midwest will meet to discuss their experiences in beginning and developing senates and associations of priests. The ten states are Minnesota, North Dakota, South Dakota, Nebraska, Iowa, Missouri, Illinois, Indiana, Michigan, and Wisconsin.

Each senate or association in the 42 dioceses in the area has been invited by the committee to send four representatives. The committee includes: Fathers Thomas P. Carroll of St. Louis, Mo.; Patrick Flood of Milwaukee, Wisc.; John McCaslin of Omaha, Neb.; James Moudry of St. Paul, Minn.; Patrick O'Malley of Chicago, Ill.; James Supple of Dubuque, Ia.; Robert Walpole of Indianapolis, Ind.; and Mel Wendrick of Detroit, Mich.

The purpose of the meeting is to exchange information so that each group may benefit from the experience of what other groups are doing, the committee indicated in their letter of invitation.

The agenda singles out three areas for discussion: structural problems of associations and senates, personnel matters, and communications.

Of the forty-two dioceses invited, thirty-eight responded, sending 123 delegates. Also in attendance were thirty-one observers from other dioceses. Summary statements regarding diocesan communications, council structures, and personnel matters were unanimously adopted. These statements, taken from the official report of the meeting, are as follows (Report, 1967).

Communications:

The necessity of communication arises from the very purpose of Priests' Senates and Associations. These bodies are established to discover the common concerns and goals of the clergy. This common purpose necessitates two-way lines of communication in many areas.

Communication must be established between Senates and Associations with the priests whom they represent. This would require that many relevant lines of communication be tried and tested to establish the clearest lines of communication.

Communication requires that the bishop listen openly to the recommendations and ideas of the Senates and Associations. The agenda of meetings with the bishop must express the concern of both the priests and bishop. Both the bishop and the Priests' Senates and Associations must be open to the common concern of all priests whom they represent. Hopefully, Senates and Associations will continue to develop new lines of communication with diocesan agencies, so that the work of Senates and Associations will influence and be influenced by these groups in each diocese.

Communication with the laity is of utmost importance if Senates and Associations are to be relevant. The 'know how' and ideas of the laity will help renew the Church as the total people of God.

Finally, communication across diocesan and provincial lines will help to clarify and encourage the roles of Priests' Senates and Associations.

Personnel:

The principles of Personnel Policy are contained in Vatican II and have been specified in documents in Chicago and St. Paul. The dignity of priests and people is of first importance in every assignment. There is a need for a personnel board for the good of the people, the morale of the priests and the competence of the bishop.

This personnel board should be elected at least in part from the total body of priests in the diocese. For the good of the Church the bishop should normally implement the recommendations of the personnel board and give reasons when he rejects their recommendations.

The personnel board should be creative in looking for new roles for the priest in the mission of the Church. They should draw on the professional advice of experts in the field of personnel, from industry, government and the private sector. Finally, adequate procedures for handling grievances should be established either by a personnel board or a separate grievance board. Confidentiality must be assured to priests who take advantage of this service.

Council Structures:

The assembled priests acknowledge the Second Vatican Council's recognition of the benefits that derive from the structural corporate effort of priests, whether it takes the form of a Diocesan Senate or an Association of Priests.

Among the benefits gained through priests' councils are an increased professional awareness among priests and more effective cooperation with the bishops in our common task of ministry in the Church.

We recognize certain means as essential to the realization of these benefits: election structures that guarantee democratic representation in deliberating bodies; committee structures that give adequate voice to the priests and assure their involvement in the activities of the council, expressing, thereby, trust in the collective competence and judgment of the body of priests; and the need for continued reexamination of existing structures to find better ways of realizing effective ministry in the Church.

Finally we recognize that priests and their councils are but one dimension of the Church of God and, consequently, we affirm and encourage the right of the laity to organize and speak freely in the Church.

Finally, the 'Committee of Eight' presented to the parliamentary session the following resolution:

> BE IT RESOLVED: That it be recommended to all Senates and Associations of the eight provinces that they support the next meeting of the priests of this region.

The Committee of Eight has a further recommendation to make to this body as a result of the opinions expressed on the evaluation sheet at lunch—and in an effort to give continuance to both the spirit and the work of this meeting. We would recommend the establishment of inter-diocesan study and action groups, these to be administered by the Committee of Eight.

Hence the Committee recommends: That the Committee of Eight establish 'ad hoc' inter-diocesan commissions for action and study of matters of concern expressed at this meeting.

Two important amendments to the above statement were proposed from the floor and unanimously adopted. They are as follows:

1. That the delegates to this convention urge their present groups to establish working relationships with such groups in other dioceses, working with the Committee of Eight.

2. That the Committee of Eight place high priority in their consideration for the establishment of one inter-diocesan commission to study the feasibility of a central clearing office for the midwest area. If feasible, such a committee would propose a plan for the financing, the personnel requirements, and the job description of such an office for formal vote at the next meeting. According to Father John Hill (1967), the meeting was full of hope. He reported little complaining about bishops' deficiencies or about the sagging morale of priests. He quoted one delegate as saying: 'Priests around the country are thirsting for this kind of experience'.

The 'Committee of Eight' asked represenatives from all the dioceses in attendance at the regional meeting to report reactions from the bishops and local councils. Thirty-eight representatives said that they had informed the bishops, but only thirteen said that their bishops were favorable, while twenty-five were uncertain. Twenty-six reported that their local councils were favorable with twelve being uncertain. Twenty-three councils favored further meetings of this type, six were uncertain, and there was no response from nine councils on this question.

On December 27 and 28, a regional meeting was held in Boston representing dioceses from New England and the Middle Atlantic states. The purpose of the meeting was similar to the Midwest regional meeting in September. A coordinating committee similar to the 'Committee of Eight' was established to conduct annual meetings for New England Senates and to act as a communication exchange.

In early winter, a questionnaire (Kennedy, 1967) was sent out to all the existing senates (approximately 130) to assess the effectiveness of the councils and to get reactions to the formation of a national organization. Sixty-five senates replied.

The data showed that most of the senates were established on the initiative of the bishop, and, foreshadowing what was to develop, most of them were set up by committees of priests independently of the chancery staff. The chancery participated in the establishment of eleven senates. Almost all of the senators were elected. Most dioceses selected members of the senate on a combination of regional and age-group bases.

The first thing that most senates did was to write a constitution to solidify their structure and purpose. Almost universally they wrote their own, without outside help or borrowing from other groups. Almost unanimously the senates felt that they had a consultative function only; four senates reported the existence of legislative functions, and, in two instances, the bishop had bound himself to accept the senate's decisions. Only ten senates felt that their function was concerned solely with priests' problems; the others felt that their area of competence involved the whole government of the diocese.

However, the structure of the various senates shows that most of their standing committees deal with problems of priests or with the continuance of the senate itself. For instance, the most numerous committees were those dealing with personnel problems and the continuing education of priests.

The easiest way to have the senate's proposal accepted by the bishop is to have him attend the senate meeting. He is present in less than one-half of the dioceses. The worst way to accomplish matters is just to send him the minutes of what took place. Another form used is a bargaining session between the bishop and the executive committee of the senate.

In twenty dioceses personnel committees have been established as a result of senate action, and separate grievance committees function in eleven dioceses, although fifteen of the twenty personnel committees include this under their competency. About one-third of the dioceses reporting have race relations committees or social action committees, but only a handful of these relate to the senate.

One-third of the dioceses answering the questionnaire have definite programs for the retirement of priests. But only eight of these were due to senate action. The favored age for retirement is seventy-five, with a few having seventy as the mandatory age.

Many obstacles to the smooth functioning of senates were cited. The most frequently mentioned were non-cooperation of diocesan officials and lack of trust of the bishop. However, other obstacles pointed to difficulties of the senate itself. Lack of committee structure and research, unfamiliarity with democratic processes and parliamentary procedure, as well as an over-crowded agenda, were often mentioned as difficulties.

The greatest successes of senates have been in facilitating communication between priests and bishop and among priests themselves. Many felt that the morale of the diocese had been raised because of the existence of the senate.

Methods of introducing items on the agenda are generally very open, with priests of the diocese, members of the senate, and the bishop enjoying equal rights. However, in about one-third of the dioceses, only senators can attend the meetings, and in almost all senates, only the senators are allowed to speak at the meeting. Minutes of the meetings are sent out by most senates to all priests in the diocese.

The questionnaire findings showed that most senates would welcome regional get-togethers of senates and associations of priests. Almost all thought that a national newsletter on senate operations would be useful. More than 75 % would see a value in a national association of priests' senates.

FEASIBILITY OF A NATIONAL ORGANIZATION

This research on the local senates, the two regional meetings, and multiple contacts with local councils convinced the 'Committee of Eight' of the need and desire for communication and collaboration on a wider scale. The Committee announced on January 17, 1968, that it was arranging a national feasibility meeting. This announcement was preceded by personal phone calls to all the provincial and diocesan contacts, informing them that such a meeting would be called. Besides discussing the improvement and efficiency of the councils' structure and work, the meeting would take up the idea of establishing a national structure for mutual assistance and the solution of felt needs.

This feasibility meeting was held on February 12 and 13, 1968. Of the 136 dioceses who had either a senate and/or association, 111 dioceses (82%) sent 298 representatives. There was a nearly unanimous approval of establishing a national organization to coordinate the work of senates and associations. The delegates also voted to expand the eight-man steering committee to twenty-nine so that all the provinces would be represented, as well as religious orders and the Eastern Rite Catholic Church. They voted to establish a national secretariat to coordinate activities and a constitutional committee to draft the constitution and bylaws for the new organization. A constitutional convention was called for May, 1968.

At a press conference following the feasibility meeting, Father Kennedy stated: 'A national organization is needed because present church law has left a vacuum. There is no means for communication between priests and their bishop.' Asked at the press conference if the U.S. bishops had given their approval for the formation of a national organization, Father Anthony Morris of Atlanta, Georgia, said: 'Actually they haven't been asked, although they were well informed in advance of this meeting'. A detailed analysis of the feasibility and constitutional meetings is given in the next chapter.

Between February 15 and May 1, the constitutional committee drew up a draft of a national constitution and bylaws. This would be the main agenda item for the May 20 convention. Five standing committees were also initiated at the February meeting. These were (1) Personnel, (2) Role of the Priest (later to be called Ministry and Priestly Life), (3) Communications, (4) Priests' Councils and Laity, and (5) Social Action (later to be called Justice and Peace). These committees were also busy with the formulation of goals and programs for the new organization.

CONSTITUTING THE NFPC

At the constitutional meeting, May 20–21, 1968, delegates from 116 dioceses voted the National Federation of Priests' Councils into existence. They approved a Constitution (see Appendix I), formally established the five standing committees, established a budget, and elected the Executive Board. Father Patrick O'Malley was elected the first president of the NFPC. Out of 126 councils present, 114 affiliated with the Federation; there were ninety-three senates and twenty-one associations.

It was significant that only one item of new business was introduced. Father John McCaslin from Omaha, Nebraska, moved that the NFPC should support the Poor People's Campaign. The motion was passed with one amendment: that the NFPC give $1,000 from its treasury to support the poor people's march.

The convention ended with the following words of Father Colin MacDonald: 'I think as we near the adjournment, we have wings; and God willing, we will fly'. And fly it did. As will be shown in the rest of this book, the NFPC started its course through the uncharted waters of collegiality. The NFPC was saying to the U.S. bishops: deal with us with respect as partners in the ministry. This was a new day both for the American priests and their bishops.

During the ensuing year, employing fatiguing but fruitful democratic procedures, the NFPC developed an agenda of concrete goals toward which to work. Initially, the emphasis was on 'interest' issues of the priests, such as priests' rights, collegial participation in governance, due process, and personnel matters. These issues created controversy with the bishops and as a consequence some of the priests' councils would disaffiliate. As will be shown in the last two chapters, this controversial aura stayed with the Federation until their Denver convention in March, 1972, when a shift in policy direction took place.

In the span of one year, from a situation where local councils were individually trying to define themselves, there was founded the beginnings of a national federation of councils. Some members would criticize the Federation for not being progressive enough. Others would be fearful and mistrusting of the leadership. Others would become so unhappy with its embroilments that they would resign from the Federation. Conservative newspapers and theologians would attack it as being disloyal to the bishops. The bishops on the whole would formally ignore it but informally would begin dialogue with its leaders.

What is of the greatest significance is that the American clergy took hold of leadership for renewing the priesthood and ministry. The Federation and its leadership gave the priests in the United States a common voice and a mechanism to initiate programs of change. The leaders weren't rebels or revolutionaries, but innovators. In their mandate for change they declared both their cooperation with, and loyalty to, the bishops. At the same time, with an autonomous organization established, priests of the country gained for themselves a new respect. They were pastoral leaders in their own right. Modern theology has pointed this out and the organization would now articulate it. There were the beginnings of a new reciprocity, no longer tilted, between the clergy and bishops. Perhaps without either group fully understanding it, the ordinary priests initiated through the Federation the first significant steps toward collegiality and subsidiarity.

In the next chapter I will discuss the structure and operations of the NFPC at the foundation stage of its development.

The Founding of the NFPC

When people are asked to join an organization, the question always come up about its worth. How effective is it? What progress is it making? How solid is its internal make up. Organizational effectiveness as a workable concept needs specification.

A framework of analyzing the effectiveness of the NFPC can be derived from the requirements an organization must meet in order to maintain itself. Social Science has specified these functional requirements or needs as goal attainment, internal and external adaptation, integration, and tension management (see Parsons, 1956).

Organizations also have a history of development. Four general stages can be identified: (1) foundation, (2) consolidation, (3) operations, and (4) achievement of goals. An organization must successfully but differentially meet the functional needs at each stage of its development. For instance, the requirements of external adaptation such as acquisition of resources are paramount in the foundation stage if the organization is to survive.

To assess the effectiveness of an organization, there is the need to specify in greater detail the functional requirements. External adaptation refers to the objective of acquiring sufficient resources such as membership size, finances, and leadership skills. Internal adaptation refers to the organization's ability to make decisions and utilize power for utilizing the proper means to reach desired goals. Integration, as an organizational objective, refers to adequate communication, collaboration, and consensus relative to the organization's activity. Tension management deals with membership morale and satisfaction with the organization's structure and operations. I include integration and tension management in the consolidation functions. Finally, goal attainment deals with specific tasks that the organization wants to accomplish. These tasks or goals must be clear, specific, and attainable. Thus, I define organizational effectiveness as the extent to which an organization makes progress toward its acquisition, consolidation, power, and goal effectiveness. An expanded treatment of this model of effectiveness together with the research techniques employed in this study is found in Appendix B.

In this chapter I will discuss the NFPC's development as an organization during the first year of its operation. In particular, I will analyze the NFPC's ability to attain its acquisition and initial consolidation requirements in terms of the organizational effectiveness framework briefly described above.

RESOURCES: MEMBERSHIP SIZE

Despite the fact that the NFPC did not have episcopal approval, 114 councils, representing 104 of the 156 dioceses (70 %), affiliated with the NFPC at the constitutional meeting in May, 1968. Within a year the affiliations grew to 134 councils, representing 114 of the 156 dioceses (73 %). Out of a total of 162 senate and association-type councils in the country, the number of senate affiliates grew from 93 to 103, and the number of association affiliates grew from 21 to 28 (a total of 83 %). The remaining three affiliates were religious order councils.

PERSONNEL SKILLS AND EDUCATION

Concerning the educational attainments of the 233 delegates present at the May, 1968, meeting, there is no data; but one can assume that all the delegates had, at minimum, both the equivalent of a B.A. degree and four years of theological training. Concerning the organizational skills of the founders and delegates, I have relied on the proceedings of three salient meetings that earmarked the foundation stage. These were the meetings held in February and May, 1968, and the convention at New Orleans which was convened in March, 1969. The New Orleans meeting is a dividing line between the foundation and consolidation phases of the organization's development. At the February meeting, I was an observer. I also utilized informal interviews employing a quota sample of thirty delegates. Although not a representative sample of the entire group,

I discovered that there was universal agreement regarding the organizational skills which went into the planning and coordinating of the agenda and convention arrangements. As one delegate said: 'This was a well-knit program—rather exhausting, but most beneficial'. Another delegate stated that he had been to many priests' conventions of various sorts but that this one was the best organized.

More information is available on the delegate leadership at the 1969 convention in New Orleans. The median age of the delegates was forty-three, and the average number of years since ordination was sixteen. Forty-one percent had earned advanced ecclesiastical or secular degrees. Forty-six percent of the delegates had come from homes characterized as white-collar. Almost half of the delegates were pastors, while 21% were diocesan officials. Delegates from urban areas represented nearly 80% of the delegates. Finally, 84% of the delegates were senators. (For an elaboration of this profile, see Stewart, 1970.) How does this profile compare with the rank and file of active diocesan priests? Koval and Bell's (1971) finding from a national sample of priests represented by affiliates to the NFPC show that the median age of the rank-and-file priest was forty-seven. Only a minority had advanced degrees. Greeley's study (1972b: 42) supports this finding, showing that only 30% of active diocesan priests had some type of advanced degree. Only 38% of the rank and file had come from white-collar backgrounds in the Koval-Bell study and only 38% of the rank and file were pastors. Finally, 80% of the clergy reported living in urban areas.

By comparison to the rank and file, the NFPC has been effective in procuring a leadership that is more energetic—manifested by its youthfulness as well as by its high levels of educational attainment—and has also had a longer experience of responsibility, evidenced by the greater proportion of pastors and diocesan officials. Finally, their white-collar backgrounds probably have afforded the delegate leadership broader social and cultural experiences during their early socialization years.

Did the delegate leadership represent the rank-and-file priests? In so far as the delegates had attained their positions through two sets of elections—namely, from the grassroots to the local council and then from the council to a delegate position—they were certainly representatives of the rank and file. But they were not representative in terms of various background characteristics. In Chapter 4, I will also show that they differed greatly from the ranks in terms of a conservative-liberal outlook.

PROCUREMENT OF FINANCIAL RESOURCES

At the constitutional meeting a budget of $135,000 was adopted for the financial period of May 20, 1968, to March 1, 1969. Of this amount, approximately 81 % was collected during this period with a balance of $47,000 on hand as of March 1, 1969. The major portion of the budget came from initiation fees and membership dues. A lower budget of $110,000 was adopted for 1969–1970 due to this surplus. During the 1970–1973 period, the NFPC was very effective in procuring the financial commitments of the affiliates. Over 87 % of the dues were paid over this period. According to Father Patrick Carney, NFPC treasurer, it is not likely that one can point to many national voluntary organizations with this kind of success.

FOUNDATION STAGE AND THE EMERGENCE OF MORALE

An important element of morale was the shared problems and needs of these delegates. Hopeful solutions to these problems seemed to lie with the formation of the NFPC. Closely akin to the common problems were the shared values held by these priest-delegates. By coming together from all parts of the country, the priests discovered that they actually had common problems and values. The evidence suggests that these elements contributed to the attractiveness of the NFPC's formation.

What were these salient problems facing the priests as a group? Analyzing the preparatory working papers and proceedings of the first two meetings, the following problems reoccur with regularity. Concerning the organization and operations of the local councils represented by the delegates, there were: (1) the lack of continuation of the senate structure after the death of the bishop; (2) the lack of participation in the decision-making process of diocesan government (collegiality); (3) insufficient communication exchanges regarding successful procedures and programs among the local councils; and, finally, (4) insufficient skills regarding the democratic process in the conduct of the senate itself.

Regarding pastoral ministries, the following problems were the most frequently discussed: (1) the lack of flexibility and experimentation for newer types of ministry due to the present authority system within the diocese, (2) clergy shortage due to lack of vocations and the resignation of priests, (3) lack of a voice in the choice of one's bishop, and (4) the lack of meaningful social action programs.

Concerning the professional role of the priests, the following problems and needs were the most salient: (1) a lack of professionalism and a consequent need for continuing education, specialization of work, and a greater autonomy and freedom in the choice and conduct of pastoral work; (2) the lack of due process needed to protect the personal and professional rights of the priest; (3) career problems such as promotions, transfers, settlement of grievances, and retirement; and (4) the lack of a dignified resignation process.

During the February meeting these problems were summarized in a position paper entitled, 'The Pastoral Ministry and Life of the Priest' (Egan, 1968). This paper was the basis of a series of workshops. Observing several of these sessions, I noted a tremendous amount of enthusiasm among the delegates. The discussions continued at a greater pace during the dinner as well as after the evening session.

On the other side of the coin were the shared values of the delegates regarding their present situation. This condition was described by one of the officials as 'an agonizing self-appraisal'. The salient values shared by the priests were also gathered from the proceedings of these meetings and from interviews with the delegates at this meeting. These values were well summarized in a major paper entitled 'National Collaboration: A Rationale' (Hill, 1968). These major values were: (1) the human right to organize; (2) greater freedom to participate in experimental ministries; (3) desire for training in secular skills; (4) desire for specialized professional competence; (5) autonomy in determining the direction and priorities of a priestly career, as well as in the setting up of standards for professional performance; (6) desire for a greater participation in the decisions of the administrative system of a diocese; (7) desire for a unifying collaboration based on democratic processes among the clergy throughout the nation; and (8) the development of norms protecting the human rights of priests, such as the freedom of conscience. The recognition that these values were shared and agreed upon by the delegates was evidenced by the standing ovation which this address received. As one delegate said afterwards: 'Father Hill said it all. There isn't any need for further comments'.

These desired states, and the problem-needs bearing upon them, were institutionalized in the formation of five major standing committees of the incipient structure of the NFPC. The committees were: (1) Personnel, (2) Role of the Priest, (3) Communication, (4) Social Action, and (5) Priests' Councils and Laity.

The interest and morale, as well as the seriousness, of the delegates were evident in my observations and in interviews with many delegates. The following statements seem to typify the cohesion present. A delegate from the Des Moines, Iowa, diocese said: 'We've participated in a tight program of work and involvement that has been absolutely fatiguing, but it's been really rewarding to all of us'. A priest from the Albany, New York, diocese said:

I'm the president of that Senate and I'm seventy years old. [Applause.] I may be on my way out and into retirement; this might be my *Nunc Dimittis*—in fact, it may have already occurred [laughter in the hall]—but I would like to speak just a word of encouragement to the younger men. I'm so happy to have lived this long, to have seen this day. There were times when I never thought such a thing could occur .... It's the greatest move the Church has made in hundreds of years. I think in the United States we're the one country that can put it over, and I hope that you will continue on with great encouragement, high ideals—and never give it up. [A spontaneous and prolonged standing ovation.]

A delegate from the Chicago Archdiocese put it this way:

I can't help but feel, and I think all of you detect it, that there is a sweep of history embracing this group. Like so many of you—and I recognize so many of the faces here—we have been on the fringe and sometimes on the inside of the things that have happened to help change the face of the Church in the United States over the past few decades. But I would say that in my time as a priest I don't remember any meeting that I feel is more significant and more historic than the gathering assembled here for these days. And if I may, I would say that from this day on, till the day you die, you are going to remember that you were present when this body of men assembled.

The great amount of expertise and energy expended by the leaders and the delegates were observed by me in many ways: (1) the businesslike air that set a tone of professionalism in the orderly conduct of the meeting, (2) the well-organized agenda and advance working papers provided for the delegates, and (3) the long hours of caucusing by the delegates on the feasibility of a national organization.

The high degree of participation and interaction was also evident at the discussion periods, workshops, caucuses, and at dinner. The layout of the convention room, with all the voting machinery and microphones, reminded me of the processes seen at a political convention. In a sense, this is what it was because, with the formation of the NFPC, democracy came knocking at the doors of the church. One observer, a magazine editor (Flaherty, 1968: 290) wrote:

It was interesting to note the growth of group cohesion as the days progressed. At lunch following the first workshops and province caucuses, it was obvious that a good bit of democratic 'debate'—if argument might not be a better word—had developed. Some of it, I gathered, had been rather free-swinging. But it was also clear that, despite the heat, lots of light had been shed on certain common problems and that a consensus on the value of some sort of national collaboration and interchange of ideas was beginning to emerge . . . . On the next day, it was pretty plain that a lot of caucusing had gone on in delegates' rooms into the small hours of the morning. There was very nearly a stampede to the floor microphones by province representatives voicing the concensus of their delegates to form a national group.

The Constitutional Convention (May, 1968), was a laborious working session. There were no major addresses. The analysis of the proceedings yielded a different emphasis of cohesion and morale. There was, indeed, a manifest enthusiasm and satisfaction, as typified by a statement of the convention chairman:

I think as we near the adjournment, we have wings; and God willing, we will fly. . . . The greatest thing that can be said about a priest is that he is all for the people of God and I think . . . this has been enhanced so much these past two days; the priests who came here are all for the people of God.

The convention was earmarked by erstwhile debate on several issues. The significant discussions concerned the following issues: (1) the use of the term 'Federation' in the title of the organization, (2) the issue of Executive Board power, and (3) the question of admitting an association to membership when its diocese also has a senate. These debates will be discussed later.

A significant point regarding this early commitment to the NFPC was the submission of a letter of intent from the local council. It implied a certain degree of courage on the part of the local council members. The reason for this is the following. The NFPC publicly stated that, though it communicated its purposes to the bishops, it neither sought nor received authorization to begin such an organization of priests. At the same time, a very prevalent value of obedience existed among most priests in the country. This involved not only following orders but also seeking permission for a course of action that would impinge on priestly activity. From the evidence of these letters of intent, signaling a certain degree of independence from the bishops, a high degree of commitment was made to the NFPC.

The attractiveness of a national organization calling for collaborative effort is caught in the following statement from a delegate from the Brooklyn, New York, diocese: 'A national organization is needed because present Church law has left a vacuum, and thus there is no means of communication between priests and their bishops about common problems'. Another delegate, from Detroit, Michigan, also cited the attractiveness of the NFPC in saying: 'Our power now is the power to present to the bishops and the laity the dignity and the position of the priesthood. When you have got a position you can talk . . . . As a priest if you want position, you work for it [*Time*, 1968]'.

In sum, the evidence suggests that the NFPC 'in becoming' had sufficiently exploited the Catholic priesthood to fashion itself as a very attractive organization.

EMERGING PATTERNS OF CONSENSUS

A high degree of consensus was evidenced in the February, 1968, meeting by the prolonged ovations of approval which met floor remarks made by the delegates on common values and problems. Other measures of agreement of the delegates were the voting patterns related to the establishment of a national organization Table 3.1 lists the ballot results based on 298 official delegates from 111 dioceses. The slightly lower total recorded reflects the fact that some delegates did not remain for this final session.

At the Constitutional Convention in May, 1968, there was a great deal of deliberation on the various sections of the constitution and bylaws. The final draft was ratified by a nearly unanimous vote. There were, however, several major disagreements preceding this ratification.

Many delegates disagreed with the term 'Federation' because it might connote unionizing; therefore they thought, for public relations, the term 'Conference' would be more suitable. Others argued that 'Federation' represents the principle of subsidiarity and local autonomy for the councils. After much debate, the term 'Federation' was retained by a vote of 147 to 75.

Executive power was the second issue of debate. The first variant stressed the freedom of movement of the Executive Board, the second stressed the accountability of the Executive Board to the House of Delegates. A proposal combining both was voted in by a large majority.

The last major issue that generated a great deal of debate concerned the membership eligibility of associations. There were two propositions: (1) associations can be members of the NFPC with voting power, even though a senate exists in the same diocese. This resolution was finally passed by a hand vote. (2) There may not be more than one priests' association represented from each diocese. A ballot vote gave the margin of 119 to 106 in favor of this proposition.

The next area of consensus concerned the work directives and priorities for the national committees. The committees on Personnel, Priests' Councils and Laity, Role of the Priest, and Social Action presented position papers on policy directives and priorities.

Table 3.1 *Voting patterns relative to issues concerning the establishment of a national organization of priests*

Question under consideration	Results of voting*	
	Yes	No
1. Should there be a national organization to coordinate the work of senates and associations?	276	1
2. Are you in agreement with the expansion of the steering committee into a 29-man ad hoc group for wider national representation?	276	5
3. Can we say that this effort towards a national organization may temporarily be referred to as a federation of priests' councils?	216	65
4. Are you in agreement with the proposed workload of this expanded committee as follows:		
a. Establish an office or secretariat to report on the Feb. 12–13 meeting, to begin communications between associations and senates on a national level, to handle all necessary coordination work?	282	2
b. Appoint a constitutional committee to draft, with the help of senates and associations, a proposed constitution?	268	14
c. Seek a general declaration of intent from all associations and senates to support the consensus of the February meeting by		
(1) cooperating in the formulation of a constitution;	267	12
(2) helping to establish specific working directions;	268	11
(3) contributing some financial support.	276	3

Table 3.1 *Continued*

Question under consideration	Results of voting*	
	Yes	No
d. Establish a date for a constitutional assembly in mid-May to which priests' councils will be asked to send delegates with power to elect a governing board, to establish affiliation, to ratify a constitution?	265	14
e. Establish working committees based on the common problem areas?	278	3

* Votes do not add up to the 298 official delegates due to abstentions.

The reports of the Personnel and of the Priests' Councils and Laity committees were accepted by the House. The Communication committee had no position paper, causing a certain amount of dissatisfaction. The work directives of the Role of the Priest and the Social Action committees were completely revamped at this convention and subsequent reports were agreed upon by the House of Delegates.

The final major item concerning the consensus processes was the election of the first president. This was the prerogative of the Executive Board. The first president, Father Patrick O'Malley, received 127 out of 206 votes on the first ballot—a clear majority. There were three candidates on the slate for president.

Analyzing the various reports and proceedings, as well as my own observation and interviews, the history of the consensus process began from a unanimous agreement on the idea of a national organization, to a nearly unanimous agreement on the ratification of the constitution, and finally to a large majority of councils agreeing to affiliate. Within the constitutional processes, as well as within work directives, however, many proposals were institutionalized by simple majorities. The evidence suggests a certain hesitancy of agreement in the following areas at the foundation stage: (1) a certain fear on the part of some that a national structure would either try to regiment the freedom of the local councils or would speak out irresponsibly on national issues, (2) some evidence of friction between senates and associations, (3) a certain uneasiness about the use of the democratic process essential to formulating the NFPC's policies and goals, and (4) a certain lack of understanding by many delegates of the realistic work directives and priorities of the Social Action Committee.

COMMUNICATION INTEGRATION

According to one informant, there was a tremendous amount of communication in terms of meetings, correspondence, and telephone calls to prepare for the national feasibility meeting. When the 'Committee of Eight' was expanded to the "Committee of Twenty-nine" at the February meeting, the communications rapidly increased, according to written reports. This committee was given three months (1) to call and to arrange for another national meeting, (2) to establish a working draft of a constitution, and (3) to develop position papers on working directives for the five standing committees. Much of this work was allocated to a wide number of delegates, but the 'Committee of Twenty-nine' had the responsibility of coordinating all the work. They prepared the initial draft of the constitution and sent it to all of the 111 dioceses represented at the February meeting. There were sixty diocesan council meetings on this initial draft. These dioceses fed back their recommendation to a Constitutional committee which, in turn, prepared a final version with alternate proposals. The evidence indicates a frenetic pace of communications among the local council representatives, the 'Committee of Twenty-nine', and the Constitutional Committee. One delegate from a midwestern diocese said: 'I've never worked and met so much in my whole life as I have during these past months. I'm glad my term is up as a representative of my council'.

FUNCTIONAL INTEGRATION AND COLLABORATION

Functional integration is the extent to which formal organizational bonds penetrate and unite the various levels and sub-units into the national organization, providing a clear definition of type and location of authority and of clarity of work tasks and general goals.

The main source of data for functional integration of the NFPC is the National Constitution and Bylaws (see Appendix A).

The structural units of the National Federation of Priests' Councils are: (1) the House of Delegates which holds the basic power to set policy; (2) the Executive Board and officers, who are responsible to the House of Delegates and who administer the programs determined by the policies adopted by the House of Delegates; (3) the committees established by the Executive Board to work on task priorities set by the House of Delegates; (4) a provincial structure established to provide a communication link between local councils and the national structure (the House of Delegates and the Executive Board).

Analyzing the constitution and informally interviewing several members of the Executive Board and one of the national officers, the evidence indicates that the structural units and linkages were sufficiently united. Furthermore, the same informants felt that there was clarity both of the types of power and duties and of their location, that is, the location of responsibility. However, concerning the work of the committees in terms of priorities and concrete programs, these same informants felt that there was much to be desired in terms of precision.

AT THE THRESHOLD OF THE FOUNDATION STAGE

In terms of a general assessment of the effectiveness of the NFPC at this stage, what does the accumulated evidence suggest? One major base line for comparison is the time factor. On August 6, 1966, a *Motu Proprio*, issued by Pope Paul VI as a result of the Vatican Council II, spelled out the general directions for the establishment of priests' councils. From that date to January, 1968, there were about 155 in operation. From May, 1967, to May, 1968, priests from across the nation began meeting together in ever-increasing numbers to consult with one another on the organization and development of their local councils. The *Motu Proprio* gave no format for procedures of the councils. The principles of democracy moved in 'to fill the vacuum'. In one year's time the first national organization of priests in the history of the Catholic Church in the United States was established, representing 70% of the dioceses. Despite the fact that this was a grassroots democratic development within a church environment accustomed neither to democratic procedures nor to inter-diocesan collaboration, the evidence suggests that the NFPC had been highly effective in bringing itself into existence.

Did it have a vibrant structure at the threshold of its existence? Yes, it did, for the NFPC had attained sufficient size and financial resources to begin to build its internal organization. It had been able to articulate the salient values and crucial problems felt by the priests across the country. It had made itself very attractive as an organization capable of understanding and doing something about the expectations of the priests. It had manifested a high degree of enthusiasm and commitment. The data describe the top leadership as providing the necessary organizational skills to develop both a high degree of involvement based on democratic participation and efficiency in work accomplishments. Lastly, the organization seemingly had adequately exploited the ideas and talents necessary to form an integrated national body and create the necessary structural units and their linkages relative to: (1) a clearly defined authority structure, (2) adequate channels of communication, and (3) sufficient research and planning committees to encompass all the salient work directives and priorities.

But the evidence also suggests certain weaknesses and limitations. There were problems of developing working relations with the bishops of the United States and of establishing concrete operational goals.

Two other problems mentioned by these informants were summed up by the President of the NFPC in the *NFPC Newsletter* (1968a):

Communication is certainly one big problem in this vast country of ours. There will have to be a flow of communications from the national organization to the local councils and then to the individual priests represented by these councils; and there will have to be just as strong a stream of communications flowing back to the national federation. The delegates will have to keep in close touch with their councils and the grassroots in order to represent them fully.

Another problem will be the attitude of priests toward the democratic process unfolding through the NFPC. Priests of the country will have to show themselves willing to accept and work in a democratic structure. Disagreements with the decisions made by the NFPC are to be expected just as in any other group acting in a democratic fashion, e.g., among the bishops at the Second Vatican Council or in their annual meetings, in local senates and associations, in a neighborhood block club. The priests of the country will have to be prepared to accept a democratic resolution of the issues presented to the NFPC.

During its first year of existence, the NFPC was active on several fronts. Much of the work was organizational in nature; communicating to local councils the nature and purpose of the NFPC; encouraging their participation; urging member councils to deliver on their financial commitments; and consolidating its consensus, collaboration, and communication networks through a series of Executive Board, national committees, and provincial meetings.

Besides acquiring new membership and working toward greater organizational consolidation, this was the time in which the NFPC began to develop concrete policy directions and program goals. These directions came primarily from the grassroots through provincial meetings of the affiliates.

Regarding the participation of rank-and-file priests at these provincial meetings, records show that over one thousand priests participated in twenty preparatory meetings. The conclusion arrived at after informal interviews of several delegates is that these provincial meetings were marked by a high degree of interest and debate. In a formal interview, the NFPC president, Father O'Malley, said the provincial structure was 'where the action is'. Furthermore, he felt that this regional mechanism was an important facilitator of communication regarding the needs and aspirations of priests and the NFPC.

Position papers containing these policy directions and goals, together with concrete resolutions, constituted the agenda for the 1969 New Orleans meeting. General areas to be covered were the role of the priests, personnel policies, priests' councils and laity, communications, and social action. The major issues that would be discussed and acted on were: (1) reform of Canon Law; (2) due process and arbitration; (3) rights of the private conscience; (4) election of bishops; (5) laicization process; (6) optional celibacy; (7) professional standards regarding training, appointment, and retirement of priests; (8) establishment of programs in communications, leadership, and sensitivity; (9) social action issues, such as the grape boycott, issues of war, and welfare rights; and (10) the Washington, D.C., and San Antonio disputes.

The NFPC engaged in one major issue during this time which received national attention. In early fall, 1968, the NFPC, through its Executive Board, responded to an appeal by the Washington, D.C., association requesting support and intervention on the occasion of the suspension of Father O'Donoghue by Cardinal O'Boyle. The issue dealt with a document issued by a number of priests which stated the rights of the private conscience on the matter of birth control. This statement was issued shortly after Pope Paul VI's letter *Humanae Vitae*. NFPC agreed to enter the case but made it clear that it was only interested in the rights of priests and the due process issues. The NFPC delegation, headed by Father Frank Bonnike, attempted to see Cardinal O'Boyle on several occasions. But he refused. Instead, the chancery office gave the committee a copy of a press release in which O'Boyle criticized the NFPC as intruders. The NFPC then requested that Cardinal O'Boyle submit to a bishops' committee on arbitration. He also refused this request. Three years later, after much damage was done to collegial relationships, the dispute was finally settled by the Vatican Congregation of the Clergy restoring to the dissenting priests their full rights. This action prompted the development of due process machinery in a number of dioceses. But the immediate effect of Cardinal O'Boyle's refusal was widespread discouragement among the Catholic clergy.

Apart from this issue, the main work of the NFPC was, on one hand, to accomplish its procurement and consolidation objectives, and, on the other hand, to begin establishing its operational goals. Only after the New Orleans convention did it move more fully into the consolidation phase and begin to mobilize for action.

AFTER ONE YEAR: ORGANIZATIONAL COHESION

The cohesion or morale of the NFPC was measured by the degree of commitment and satisfaction with the policies, conduct, and management of the organization. Data reported in this section was gathered from a questionnaire administered to the delegates at the New Orleans convention in March, 1969. The data speak for the organizational climate at this stage of development. The findings are based on a 67% return rate.

Ninety percent of the New Orleans delegates were highly committed to the organizational policies of the NFPC and 78% expressed satisfaction with the organizational management of the federation over the past year. While almost 70% of the delegates were generally satisfied with the conduct and direction of the New Orleans meeting, there was conflict concerning several resolutions. In particular, representatives from associations wanted to dispatch the prepared agenda and open the meeting to the morality of the Vietnam war, race and poverty issues. This move was beaten down.

The controversial resolutions passed by the convention, such as calling for due process of priests' rights and the consideration of optional celibacy (see Chapter 6), were met with some anger, ambivalence, and hesitancy among a small percentage of delegates. One must keep in mind that the NFPC calls for both the formulation and *implementation* of policy goals. In short, it calls for a commitment to action. As the president of the NFPC stated: 'The priests-delegate must learn to confront their bishops with the gutty issues that affect the lives and work of their fellow priests'.

On the whole, however, the evidence suggests that the NFPC had been able to consolidate itself very well, during its first year of existence, as an attractive organization. It was earmarked by a great amount of participation and by the employment of democratic processes through which common grassroots problems and aspirations were relayed to the national structure through the provincial meetings. The main problem with the democratic processes, however, was stated by the president of the NFPC in a formal interview. He said:

The rank and file priests are not accustomed to democratic procedures. They do not trust their elected delegates sufficiently to empower them to speak officially for the local council in such a way that the resolutions adopted by the delegates become binding policy directives. When the delegates go back to their own dioceses, there is a certain loss of commitment to and enthusiasm for the NFPC. Many grassroots priests, in effect, are saying at present: 'You have no power to speak for us'. We are a rather spirited group when we are together at a plenary session, but we lose a great deal of this when we go back home. We are effective on the national meeting level and even more so at the regional structure level in terms of communication, involvement of the fellows and dedication. Our main problem is the individual delegate's performance on the local council level. There he is isolated.

ORGANIZATIONAL CONSENSUS

The NFPC's resolutions were specifications of the general policy directions adopted for the forthcoming year. In other words, the resolutions embody the operational goals of the NFPC. All the proposed resolutions were adopted by at least a simple majority. There were a cluster of social action resolutions which were returned to committee to be reworked. They were subsequently passed. However, 43 % of the delegates expressed complaints about the handling of these particular resolutions.

There was total agreement and confidence in the presidential leadership. Father O'Malley was unanimously re-elected for a second term. The high degree of consensus regarding the resolutions passed at the convention was indicated by 70 % delegate approval.

By and large, the New Orleans meeting was a success in mustering together diverse clergy backgrounds and attitudes into a unifying spirit filled with energy and hope. This meeting was highly symbolic of a charged collegial spirit which provided a much needed impetus to the NFPC during its first full year of activity.

ONGOING COMMUNICATION

During the first year of operations, one of the major focuses of the NFPC was the development of sufficient channels of communication and their effective use. The vast majority of the House of Delegates (81%) reported that they felt that they were sufficiently well informed on the activities of the NFPC.

The president of the NFPC stated in an interview that, at that time, he saw the function of the national structure to be that of a communication center providing the service of information exchange and of a national voice for priests to communicate to the bishops the problems of the priests and the needs of the church. He further said:

We are not a social action force at present and I do not see that we are in the position to act as a professional association which can set standard of excellence relative to the pastoral ministry. I hope we can come to these things but we are not there as yet. What we can do now is research the problems facing the priests and publicize these facts. We can also publicize the efforts and successes of local councils for more effective action programs. But presently communications is our big concern. We [the Executive Board] are in close contact with the presidents of local councils. The major problem is reaching the grassroots priests. This is by far the greatest problem. But it is a problem that the local councils must solve.

I have noted the general satisfaction of the delegates concerning the communications from the national structure to the local councils. What about communications up to the national level? In the same interview with the president of the NFPC, he stated that the national office and Executive Board felt that the feedback from the local councils was greatly in need of improvement. At this time, the only effective grassroots communication was through the provincial meeting.

In summary, the evidence suggests that the communication channels and their use were adequate in terms of the downward flow. The upward flow needed much improvement. The major problem, according to the evidence, was the communications and 'public relations' between the local councils and their rank-and-file priests regarding the purposes of the NFPC. Lastly, the most effective communication mechanism between the national structure and the local councils was the provincial meeting.

COLLABORATION

Earlier in this chapter I reported that the powers and work tasks were clearly delineated, providing the basis for a well-functioning organization. The work of the NFPC was greatly clarified and specified at the New Orleans meeting. How was the work handled during the first year of operation?

Analysis of records and interviews of officers depict the following sequence. After the 1968 session, the work tasks and directives went to the national committees. They handled the material in liaison with the Executive Board. Each national committee was responsible for formulating resolutions. Suggestions from local councils were sought concerning the work directives. Then the committees went to the regional meetings with their proposals. The regional meetings reworked the proposals, adding new business. This information came back to the committees and Executive Board, who fashioned the materials into resolutions and provided guidelines for implementation. The final draft went to all local councils for review and comments. Based on these feedbacks, the final product became the agenda for the New Orleans convention. This was the general work process employed during the past year. The informants stated, however, that these processes were not completely successful. For instance, only twenty of the twenty-seven provinces had regional meetings. Many reports and minutes from the regions were tardy, as well as some reports from the committees to the Executive Board. As a result, the final informational materials for the convention were sent late to the local councils. This did not allow the delegate a great deal of time to discuss the agenda with the council representatives. Subsequently, the NFPC has remedied this situation by scheduling all provincial meetings before December 1 of each year. Nevertheless, as I stated earlier, 78% of the delegates were satisfied with the NFPC's management during the past year.

SUMMARY

The degree of satisfaction (78 %) with the management of the NFPC during the first year manifests a high degree of collaboration. The commitment to the policy resolutions and their urgency (90 %) indicates a strong solidarity and cohesion. A great majority of the delegates (81 %) felt that they were well informed. Consensus on the convention's resolutions, taken as a whole, was 70 % of the delegate population. All things considered, this was a remarkable indication of how well the organization had consolidated itself, especially around the definitional crisis of the priesthood. For instance, delegates manifested an overwhelming agreement on those resolutions touching on their rights as priests (93 %) and the legal definitions of their pastoral work as found in church law (85 %). This consensus implies that the role crisis of the priesthood was the foremost problem in the minds of the priests.

4

Who are the Leaders?: 'An Uncomfortable Company'

Who is a liberal? Generally one thinks of a person who has belief in and commitment to policies of change and methods of innovation which have as their common purpose both the development of greater toleration and respect for the rights and freedoms of those differing from others. In other words, a liberal is one who views various types of pluralism as normative. In practice the liberal dislikes arbitrary authority and is open to many points of view.

The liberal is not of one piece. A person may be liberal on political issues of civil liberties but conservative regarding economic or religious tenets. The data from my studies show that the NFPC's House of Delegates are more liberal, open to change and democratic than the rank and file priests across the nation. See Stewart (1971) for complete documentation.

I particularly want to discuss several issues dealing with decision making and power which concerned the NFPC. The first issue of renewal dealt with the election of the Pope. The delegates by 81% compared to 69% of the grassroots clergy preferred the election of the Pope by an international council of bishops instead of the present college of cardinals. This finding clearly indicates that the NFPC leaders wished to broaden the base of power and decision making.

Regarding episcopal elections or rather selections, while the delegates (51%) compared to the rank and file (28%) felt priests' councils should participate in the decision making process, the diocesan pastoral council was considered the most salient power group. The reason why 66% of the delegates as compared to 36% of the ranks favored this group is clearly the representativeness of its membership within the dioceses, thus providing greater assurance for democratic participation.

The delegates (68%) compared to 41% of the ranks favored the involvement of the local priests' council in the appointment of pastors, thus opposing the procedure of the bishop making these decisions solely by himself.

It has been six years since this study was completed and today, due to the endeavors of the NFPC, most dioceses have personnel boards which have significant power in the appointment decisions.

Regarding issues of due process for priests, personnel matters, change of the celibacy law, deletion of mandatory Sunday Mass obligation, and management of diocesan finances, the delegates compared to the rank and file favored by wide percentages both a liberalization of these issues and an increased participation of other diocesan groups in their deliberations.

Possible explanations for this contrast between the liberal NFPC delegates and the moderate-conservative rank and file are the delegates' background factors such as youthful age, higher levels of education, higher rates of parents in mixed marriages, all of which may have a contributing influence on the delegates working for greater tolerance, participation, and change. One other important influence, namely, the delegates' status in the diocesan council and the federation provides both a certain amount of power as well as an accumulation of vast amounts of information. Receiving new ideas, controversial proposals, et cetera, develop a liberalizing influence and provide a certain rationale if not power to be bold and daring. It is clear that this process has been operating when one examines the resolutions of the first four NFPC conventions.

One must remember that this is the first real taste of power and democracy for priests since Bishop England's experiment in the early nineteenth century.

However, the aftermath of Vatican II left the rank and file priests bewildered, powerless, and paralyzed. They have been on the periphery of the diocesan governing process. One respondent in the study summed it up this way:

I believe that most of our problems as a Church stem from a weakening of faith both among the clergy and the laity. Uncertainty about Christ, sacraments, the after-life, the function of a church, have bred apathy in the laity and inertia or frustation or hostility or cynicism among an increasingly large number of the clergy.

In short, many rank-and-file priests have grown accustomed to waiting for changes to come from the top. They are not familiar with the idea that the renewal of the priesthood can come about by a democratic process and initiative represented by the local councils. Hence many priests have isolated themselves or have been isolated from the renewal process and routinely accept almost anything that comes from the chancery office. They have not been asked to share in the decision-making process of the diocese. They are not close to communication exchanges which might expose them to fresh ideas. For further information on these differences, see Stewart (1972).

It was during this malaise that a handful of priest leaders forged a new concept and a new structure. The NFPC would be for some years an agent of change, a thorn in the side of the bishops. But without it I am convinced that much of the modernization of Catholic Church USA would not have taken place.

I will now examine the internal leadership structure of the NFPC. Here one will find tensions, conflicts, and contrasts which, I believe, have been beneficial to this federation as an agent of new ideas and innovations.

'AN UNCOMFORTABLE COMPANY'

Between 1969 and 1972, I conducted two studies evaluating the effectiveness of the NFPC (Stewart, 1969b and 1972). NFPC's House of Delegates were asked, among a variety of questions, to take a careful look at the properties of the federation as an organization without considering where it stood on church-related issues. Each study had a return rate of over 89 %, providing a highly accurate picture of the total delegate membership. This membership is divided into two major groups: senate and association members. For the sake of brevity, the total NFPC members will be referred to as TM, association members as AM, and senate members will be designated by SM. This data will be the basis for discussions in this and the following chapter.

I related several important factors together as a unit, such as pastors, older priests, those satisfied with episcopal leadership. A general trend emerged in which the SM reflected attitudes of these groups while the AM reflected attitudes of their counterparts. Specifically, the uppermost concerns of the AM were issues of civil rights, peace, social action, lay participation, and other 'value' issues of the common weal; the SM were more concerned with 'interest' issues of personnel policies, inter-council communications, and professional standards. While both AM and SM are change oriented, the AM are much more so. They are viewed not only by the bishops but also by their senate colleagues as the militants of this priest movement.

The most likely explanation for the AM being more militant and change-oriented is the fact that they were more dissatisfied with episcopal leadership and the slow pace of renewal. Most of the AM were ordained during or immediately after the Vatican Council II. They internalized the high expectations for change stemming from the Council. They also experienced rising expectations of social justice and equality for all due to the massive federal legislation on race and poverty enacted during this period. Seventy-five percent of the AM compared to 45 % of the SM indicated they felt it important that the church commit itself to helping solve the problems of race and poverty.

Because they experienced some initial victories of church renewal and governmental commitment to social justice, the AM became increasingly militant when the pace of change finally slowed. By 1972 85 % of the AM compared to 67 % of the SM indicated the need for greater clerical militancy in solving societal problems.

The AM certainly feel that militancy is a very important tool to create a more effective NFPC. The AM probably feel that respectful confrontation will gain respect for the NFPC from a clergy who are accustomed to the ecclesiastical rituals of paternalism, humility, and obedience. It is clear that there is an underlying dynamic between the more and less progressive units within the delegate leadership; it is as if there is a two-party system operating on the basis of 'value' and 'interest' orientations. Although these orientations are a matter of degree between the AM and SM, they do make a consistent and significant pattern of differences within the NFPC. This difference is evident in the degree of the SM's and AM's commitment to the NFPC's activities and objectives. One must recall that the very founding of the NFPC was controversial; moreover, the early years of the NFPC's activity were marked by confrontation with the bishops over the rights of priests. This perspective and action approach were more akin to the outlook of AM than of SM.

The dynamic of these two major orientations provides the NFPC with a healthy combination of stability and innovation, balance and flexibility, as well as maintaining a power balance between the two as the years have gone by. However, the SM has become ascendant. The militant association chapters have begun to fold. The years from 1974 through a good portion of 1976 have become for the NFPC ones of greater cooperation and accommodation to the Catholic bishops. The associations, being fewer in number and calling for greater militancy, were always vulnerable. For instance, at the Denver convention in 1972, the House of Delegates voted down a two-part resolution commending the associations and directed the NFPC's Executive Board to communicate this to the NCCB and secondly to insist that all provincial groups include associations. Despite this antagonism, or perhaps because of it, the NFPC has served well both as a model of democratic processes and forums for debate.

Backgrounds of the Delegates

A sizeable majority of both delegate populations were involved in parish work, and the trend is toward greater involvement in the pastoral ministry. In 1972, 75% compared to 67% of the TM in 1969, were involved in parish work. This is an 8% increase. The parish involvement of the AM, however, grew 14% during this time. Within this trend there was a sharp rise of associate pastor representatives, increasing 15% by 1972. The pastor's representation remains the same for the TM, but there was a decline of diocesan officials as delegates, dropping 16%. It is clear that the NFPC delegate leadership in 1972 was more reflective of the grassroots than in 1969. This has had implications for NFPC policy during the ensuing years. The delegates, as we shall see later on, become more concerned about the pastoral and social 'value' issues, and less concerned about the 'interest' issues of priests' rights and prerogatives.

In terms of being satisfied with their work and also with episcopal leadership, the delegates manifest two contrasting trends. The TM are more satisfied with their work in 1972 (98%) than in 1969 (81%). The AM have become more satisfied with their work, increasing 16% (from 81% in 1969 to 97% in 1972). This is due, in no small part, to the increased liturgical experimentation and social action ministries. On the other hand, there is a high degree (55%) of delegates' dissatisfied with episcopal leadership, with 80% of the AM unhappy with this leadership.

What accounts for these inverse trends? The sociological principle of relative deprivation may shed some light on this phenomenon. Since 1965, priests have been making small gains and improvements both in terms of their ministry and their status in the authority structure of the diocese. But in comparison to expectations held out by the Vatican Council for modernization and the actual implementation on the diocesan level brought about greater clerical dissatisfaction. At the same time, however, priests were becoming more satisfied with what they could do in the ministry, especially in the liturgy and in the social apostolate. Thus, the delegates were more satisfied than before with their work but became increasingly dissatisfied with episcopal leadership.

In terms of advanced educational attainments, the TM72 are better educated than the TM69 in terms of both ecclesiastical and secular degrees and the AM are better educated in both of these areas than the SM.

In terms of parental educational background, the TM72 have parents who are significantly better educated than the parents of the TM69. Finally, the TM72 come from homes that are more white-collar in nature as compared to the TM69 who are over-represented by blue-collar homes. In sum, the 1972 delegates seem to reflect more middle class backgrounds while their 1969 counterparts come from traditionally Catholic strongholds—the working class.

The TM69 and TM72 state that their parents' political views are, for the most part, moderate to conservative (93% for both sets of parents). By contrast, the delegates themselves are much more liberal politically and socially than their parents. Moreover, they are more liberal in 1972, with 65% of the TM compared to 55% of the TM69 embracing this orientation. As might be expected, the AM

(87%) are more liberal than the SM (59%) by a range of 28%.

In summary, there are distinct trends in the House of Delegates over this four-year period. The delegates of 1972 are more involved in parish work, as indicated by the increase of associate pastors as delegates. Most of the delegates come from urban areas. In 1972, the TM are more satisfied with their work and much less satisfied with the episcopal leadership than their 1969 counterparts. The AM are more marked on these trends than the SM. The 1972 TM in general and AM in particular are slightly younger than the 1969 delegates. Likewise, the 1972 TM are slightly better educated than their 1969 counterparts. More TM72 than TM69 come from white-collar homes. While the parents' political views are much more moderate, the delegates themselves are much more liberal and increasingly so over the four-year period, with the AM more liberal than the SM.

What can be concluded from this analysis of the NFPC leadership about the future direction of the NFPC? First, in terms of change itself, I would expect more change in the direction, definition, and types of pastoral ministries. For instance, a pastor from the West Coast stated that the NFPC has influenced his council to be more concerned with parish issues.

This change would also involve a greater inclusion of the social ministry as part of the pastoral ministry and a shift of emphasis away from issues revolving around priests' personnel policies. These latter battles have been fought and won. I would also expect the approach of the NFPC to be more diplomatic and sophisticated in dealing with the NCCB, but, paradoxically, more militant in dealing with wider social causes. I would also expect the senate delegates to become more militant regarding these social justice issues. These issues lie beyond the circle of episcopal authority. Priests, with due process a reality, feel more free to get involved in social justice.

At the same time, I would expect certain controversial issues, defined as implicating the bishops' authority, to be realistically assessed in terms of strategy and placed on the back burner at least for the present. These is no doubt in my mind, however, that in time pressure will build up on such issues as women priests, homosexuality as a normative option, married priests, and birth control. If a reference group tells us anything at all, it certainly shows very clearly how ecumenical activity carries the price of normative change for Roman Catholics.

Other types of controversial issues, especially in the area of justice such as corporation ethics, unionization of farm workers, urban and rural poverty, et cetera, will be emphasized. Finally, I would expect the NFPC to continue with caution to move forward with an agenda for change, without the official support and legitimacy from the bishops.

Development of the NFPC Organization

Seventy-five percent of both TM69 and TM72 feel that the vacuum in ecclesiastical leadership (bishops and pope) has been an important factor in the development of the NFPC. About 67% of the TM69 and TM72 feel that both the lack of episcopal consultation with priests and violation of priests' rights were also important influences. The fourth reason was the lack of official church commitment in solving the problems of race, poverty, and peace. Lastly, the celibacy issue was of little importance in establishing the federation. This last issue was the least important influence in the formation of the federation. Another factor mentioned by many respondents was the usefulness of the NFPC as an exchange of communication. A Milwaukee pastor sums up this view by stating: 'The desire to exchange information and cooperate with other senates in united action is why we joined the NFPC'.

Of all these issues, a much greater percentage of the AM69 and AM72 feel that these issues are important than do their senate member counterparts. As observed earlier, the AM are much more liberal and more dissatisfied with ecclesiastical leadership than are the SM. It is also important to note that the association membership is the organizational component which consistently swings the NFPC into a more progressive path regarding policy issues and resolutions. But, being a numerical minority within the House of Delegates, it is easier to understand why it has been more difficult to implement these policies on a wide scale back in the home dioceses.

In terms of making the NFPC more effective, 89% of the TM69 feel that the bishops' recognition of the NFPC is important, compared with only 74% of the TM72. While more SM72 (80%)

than AM72 (56%) think that recognition is important, both think that it is less important than do their 1969 counterparts. More delegates seemingly have become used to their unofficial, if not deviant, status.

However, 62% of the TM72, compared with only 39% of the TM69, feel that it is important for the NFPC's effectiveness to publicly declare its loyalty to the bishops. Greater support for the importance of this factor is found with both the 1972 AM and SM. Yet, the use of militancy as an effective instrument is more widely accepted by the TM72 (72%) than by the TM69 (56%), with a greater percentage of AM72 (85%) than SM72 (69%) feeling this way.

The picture of the 1972 NFPC is one which the leadership feels more secure in relation to the bishops' judgment toward the NFPC. A greater percentage of the leadership feels that, on the one hand, it would help the organization's effectiveness if it made a public declaration of loyalty to the bishops; on the other hand, the use of greater militancy also would lead to organizational effectiveness. I interpret these responses as depicting a leadership which is beginning to feel more at home with power and more autonomous in its relationship with the bishops. In other words, being tough-minded in strategy assumes a certain degree of leadership security, but it doesn't exclude loyalty to those who have power.

In summary, the NFPC is clearly a response to certain structural inadequacies within the post-conciliar church: leadership is wanting, authority is too inflexible and threatened, communication is inadequate. The clergy, not used to exercising authority and leadership independently of their bishops, found themselves in 1969 a bit insecure and uncomfortable with power. With experience and mutual support, the 1972 leadership is more secure and confident. Feeling relatively deprived when they compared progress with expectations, the 1972 leadership became more restive, yet more reflective and mature regarding its agenda for change. The NFPC leadership of the earlier period necessarily dramatized the issues and pointed to the hurting conditions, e.g., due process issue in the Washington, D.C., case and the 'Moment of Truth' statement. As beneficiaries of this necessary activity, the 1972 leadership began on a path of greater diplomacy.

Its new policies and directions deal with issues, which are current, yet not impinging on the bishops' authority. Thus, the NFPC's agenda for 1973 emphasized the theme of pastoral accountability. As will be shown in Chapter 7, after the 1972 Denver convention, the NFPC began to emphasize pastoral responsibility and reconciliation as well as spiritual aspects of the ministry as the basis of hope for people suffering social and economic injustices.

PROFESSIONALISM AND THE PRIESTHOOD

There are several qualities characterizing a profession such as the ministry, medicine, and law. I asked the delegates how they compared themselves to doctors and lawyers in terms of these qualities. On the whole, a greater percentage of the TM72 than the TM69 consider themselves as much of a professional as a doctor or lawyer. While 65 % of the TM69 feel that they have comparable depth of professional knowledge, 76 % of the TM72 feel that they have this knowledge. About 74 % of both the TM69 and TM72 feel personal responsibility for their work. Most of the delegates feel they don't have professional autonomy. This is not surprising for a hierarchical organization which tends to centralize and concentrate authority at the top. Only 62 % of the TM72 feel that they are guided by a professional code of conduct compared with 60 % of the TM69. Lastly, 89 % of the TM72 feel that they have a professional commitment to serving people, compared with 84 % of the TM69. What accounts for this growing professional awareness?

The growth in the delegates' perception of professionalism is no doubt due to the development of the NFPC organization. Before the NFPC was established in May, 1968, there was no forum for priests to discuss their status and attendant rights and obligations. In its discussions, the NFPC provided the opportunity for priests to look at themselves from a perspective different from the then current doctrinal and canonical definitions. The reason why the SM, more than the AM, view themselves as professionals is probably due to the 'interest' issues which had priority in the senates during this time especially personnel matters. The concern of the AM is not so much the professional status issues but the issues of community justice and equality. No doubt the AM feel that the NFPC organization is an important tool to assist the clergy in its professional growth and its grievances but, more importantly, it was formed to assist in the area of social justice.

'VALUE' AND 'INTEREST' ORIENTATIONS

A 'value'-oriented person expects rights or accepts duties in generalized terms independently of his particular relationship to the other person or group. 'Interests' refer to special rights and to an allocation of goods which particular individuals or groups desire (LaPalombara, 1964).

Movements for change will vary and take different directions depending on whether the participants are 'value'-oriented or 'interest'-oriented. The 'value'-oriented outlook, as I am employing it, is closely linked to Mannheim's (1946) concept of Utopia, namely, ideas that stir people to break away from the existing order to bring about a greater societal good; 'interests' are related to his concept of ideology, which is a set of ideas that support the commitment to present arrangements. Turner and Killian (1957: 331–85) summarize this by stating that 'value'-oriented movements point in the direction of changing a social institution for the greater common good. These organizations are concerned with societal reform rather than personal reward. Movements of self-interest, which they call power-oriented movements, are directed more toward gaining some recognition or special status. The incentives of 'interest'-oriented actors are the approval of the people that they either love, fear, or respect. 'Interest'-oriented actors take action, but such action must always be calculated in terms of personal or group gains and losses. Their operating principle is to act with caution and not ignore those who have the power (Neal, 1965: 45–54). A study by Nelson (1964) supports the relationship between 'values' and 'interests' and types of change. He found that individuals who defined the church in terms of the local congregation's interests were more resistant to a church merger than those who defined the church in 'value' terms, such as the 'Communion of Saints'.

I turn now to the question of 'value' and 'interest' orientations as they relate to both the AM and SM and to the pastoral reform goals of the NFPC.

The AM consider both the freedom of conscience and the right to dissent much more meaningful than the SM. In the two studies (Stewart, 1969b and 1972), AM (77%, 77%), as compared to SM (51%, 62%), maintain a strong attachment to freedom of conscience in their roles as priests. Also, the AM (84%, 83%), as compared to SM (48%, 55%), strongly adhere to the right to dissent. This pattern holds regarding other 'value' commitments: (1) the right to protect one's reputation, (2) social justice, and (3) spiritual values.

We are discovering here, as well as in other findings, that the AM and SM show a pattern of differences in the intensity and scope of 'values' and 'interests'. I am not assuming that 'values' and 'interests' orientations are mutually exclusive categories. The AM, however, are characterized chiefly as 'value'-oriented and use 'values' as a basis for seeking change, while SM are primarily 'interest'-oriented and use 'interests' as the basis for their strategy of change. The two studies show that SM (90%, 80%) are more 'interest'-oriented, as compared to AM (87%, 56%). For instance, the SM feel that it is quite important that the NFPC obtain recognition from the NCCB. Also, 41% and 68% of the SM, as compared to the AM (26%, 41%), feel that it is of importance to have the NFPC publicly declare its loyalty to the NCCB.

Turning to the relationship of 'values', 'interests', and pastoral change, the 'value'-oriented AM are more at home with pastoral change together with a militant approach than the 'interest'-oriented SM. Part of this is due to the 'value' orientations which are directed to the common good in contrast to special interests and part is due to the change-oriented nature of the associations. See Stewart (1973b) for an elaboration of these two dimensions.

Summary and Conclusions

The associations are better predictors of pastoral change and militant orientation than are the SM. The AM are more 'value'-

oriented while the SM are more 'interest'-oriented. These relationships taken together manifest a consistent pattern of differences between the AM and SM.

The NFPC is a combination of two distinct organizations and perspectives. From what the data have told us and what was stated earlier about the NFPC's failure to approve and affirm by convention resolution its own association members, it is clear there are inner tensions. The AM are less interested in and less cautious about their relationship to the bishops' authority. They see certain episcopal directives as narrowing the limits of freedom and blunting the modernization process that started with Vatican Council II. With these sanctions operative, one can expect a variety of adaptations on the part of the 'value'-oriented AM. The following alternatives seem theoretically plausible for the association members: (1) create a new national structure which would include associations only; (2) stay with the NFPC and press for strong innovative approaches; and (3) possibly disintegrate. What course of action the AM has been following through the years of 1974 through 1976 is disintegration by attrition.

It takes a great deal of organizational and personal strength to weather the pressures of being 'deviant' in the eyes of the bishops and also your colleagues especially when many of the early controversial issues have been settled. Associations will die, and this will have a profound effect on the direction of the NFPC. Unless sufficient number of senates become 'radicalized' or a sufficient number of 'avant garde' religious order councils affiliate, the NFPC will lose that creative balance of stability and change, a reciprocity for change upon which it was founded.

Putting the NFPC Together
for Power and Performance

CONSOLIDATING THE FEDERATION

I will discuss the problems facing the NFPC in bringing senates, associations, and religious order councils together for national collaboration. My main questions concern how well the NFPC has put itself together over this four-year period and how well it has performed in reaching its goals defined by its convention resolutions. In this analysis, I will employ the model of effectiveness briefly discussed in Chapter 3. An expanded version of this model as well as the research techniques for this study is found in Appendix II.

The reader will recall that every organization has four social requirements it must successfully meet in order to maintain itself and survive: adaptation to its competitive environment, integration of its internal operations, cohesion or morale and commitment, and achievement of its goals. An organization also has a certain career which involves a sequence of movements through several stages: foundation, consolidation, operational, and goal achievement. In the consolidation stage it must meet the requirements of integration and membership's commitment while still paying attention to acquisition of resources. The analysis of the NFPC in this section will be concerned with the following aspects of consolidation effectiveness: (1) collaboration and synchronization of tasks, (2) organizational consensus, (3) communication structures and functions, and (4) cohesion or loyal commitment of the membership. I will also discuss power and performance of the NFPC.

During the four-year period from 1969 through 1972, the NFPC was only moderately effective in establishing the routines which go with a complex division of labor and in developing an efficient well-synchronized organization. While 74% of the 1972 TM compared to only 56% of the 1969 TM gave high marks for establishing the necessary organizational structures, about 60% of the delegates over both time periods felt the NFPC was running smoothly. In particular, the communication structures and flow of information from the NFPC through the local diocesan councils to the grassroots priests was in trouble. While 49% of the 1969 TM noted strains and problems with communications between the NFPC and its affiliates, only 31% of the 1972 TM felt there were these problems.

At the same time an overwhelming majority ranging from 79% to 93% of both sets of delegates were in agreement of the NFPC's policy and purposes as well as the proper allocation of power to the officers and the House of Delegates. Organizational consensus was quite high in the initial years.

At the outset in 1969 the NFPC had been highly successful in attaining its cohesion objective measured by commitment, satisfaction, morale and harmony among the members. But over this four-year period, it has not sustained the morale of the members at the same high level. In particular the AM became more disenchanted with the NFPC. See Table 5.1.

The general picture one can draw from these findings is that initially and absolutely, the NFPC has been fairly successful in consolidating the minds (consensus) and hearts (cohesion) of its membership than in consolidating organizational behavior measured by coordination of work and communication flow. In other words, it has been easier to accomplish unity of attitudes than unity of effort. Commitment and agreement to a new idea, such as the NFPC, doesn't necessarily translate into consolidated efforts especially at the local level. Council affiliates always have had a certain ambivalence about the NFPC. The affiliates needed the NFPC and its expertise, knowledge, and symbolic power but back in the home diocese, many senates would make efforts to dissociate themselves with the federation except when the NFPC's symbolic power was used to the advantage of the local council in negotiations with the bishop.

But when one looks at the changes in these consolidating factors over time, a somewhat different pattern emerges. The NFPC was becoming more effective in both the development of its work and communication structures and the carrying out of these tasks. It was becoming less effective in maintaining consensus regarding the NFPC's authority, maintaining membership satisfaction, and building organizational harmony. The summary Table 5.1 provides an overall picture of consolidation effectiveness.

As time went on, the NFPC became less effective in improving the satisfactions and commitments among the delegates, especially the 1972 AM. But, as mentioned, it improved its effectiveness relative to collaboration and communication processes. This points to processes which usually develop over time with newly formed organizations. A routinization of zeal and commitment sets in, together with a bureaucratization of procedures. Efficiency competes with enthusiasm and change. Although an organization can have both, standardization seeks a certain stability at the expense of change which might cause controversy.

One possible reason for the AM's growing disenchantment with the NFPC was the gradual shift of emphasis and direction. The due process goal had been virtually attained in every diocese. Social justice programs and experimental ministries were increasingly emphasized. For these reasons, the AM72, in absolute terms, still registered high on morale and consensus. But the NFPC began to turn away from the issues of participatory democracy and redistribution of ecclesiastical power. These 'value' issues were of great importance to the AM. The NFPC also began to give greater attention to less dramatic matters, such as continuing education, parish management, and spiritual renewal. These were more relevant to the SM than the AM.

The NFPC is a good working example of the democratic process. Two affiliates, different in structures, purposes, and ideology have proven, though not without strains, they can operate within one body. The positive benefits to the NFPC and the priesthood in general are clear. The one group provides the stability and continuity needed for organizational success; the other provides the innovation and change necessary for growth. Depending on how one looks at the organization over time, there is much consensus and dissent, commitment and indifference, coordination and confusion. The NFPC will need to continue its efforts to consolidate itself with the local level. When in session, the House of Delegates operates quite smoothly. But the NFPC is more than an annual meeting. One of the organizational challenges that the NFPC faces is building links with the grassroots. I will now discuss power and performance of the NFPC.

Table 5.1   *Evaluation of the dimensions of consolidation effectiveness by council members (reported by percentages)**

	1969			1972			
	TOTAL delegates (N=203)	Senators (N=169)	Association members (N=30)	TOTAL delegates (N=186)	Senators (N=140)	Association members (N=34)	VARIATION OF TM
COLLABORATION							
Work routine of Executive Board	56	54	63	74	75	74	18
Work routine of the House	57	53	82	66	66	65	9
Smooth running	56	53	70	63	61	67	7
COMMUNICATION							
Adequacy of networks	35	33	39	42	35	67	7
Information flow from NFPC	55	53	64	55	50	73	0
Communication strains†	49	50	48	31	31	35	−18
CONSENSUS							
NFPC's objectives and policies	89	87	100	93	93	94	4
Authority of Executive Board	87	85	100	83	80	91	−4
Authority of House	88	86	94	87	85	91	−1
Decisions by House	83	80	94	85	86	81	2
Adequacy of procedures	79	76	93	81	81	82	2

COHESION

	1969			1972			
Identity and commitment with aims	87	85	100	68	66	74	−19
Organizational satisfaction	77	74	90	65	64	68	−12
Organizational harmony	86	84	94	74	73	78	−12

* These percentages represent the positive evaluations of delegates. The negative responses are not presented for the purpose of clarity.
† The decrease in strains of coordinating communications indicates an increase of effectiveness.

Table 5.2 *Evaluation of NFPC's influence on outside groups by council members (reported by percentages)**

	1969			1972			
	TOTAL delegates (N = 203)	Senators (N = 169)	Association members (N = 30)	TOTAL delegates (N = 186)	Senators (N = 140)	Association members (N = 34)	VARIATION OF TM
On the diocesan bishop	19	21	7	28	31	17	9
On the NCCB	20	18	30	35	34	37	15
On the local council	51	50	51	53	51	64	2

* Percentages represent only the positive evaluations. The negative evaluations of the delegates are not presented for the purpose of clarity.

POWER OF THE FEDERATION

Power is the capacity of an organization to mobilize resources for the attainment of its goals. Power is exercised through decision-making positions and organizational mechanisms. These decisions involve several different organizational issues, such as technical, managerial, and policy areas.

Power is relational in nature. The power relationship within an organization is based on mutual dependency of its various substructures. Although power is often viewed within an interpersonal framework, that is, from the perspective of leadership influence, I wish to discuss power as an organizational activity.

Power can be viewed as a manipulative and coercive force or as a legitimate influence. This latter type of power is called authority. Authority involves the acceptance of the system of power when one affiliates with the organization. Accepting the values and policies of a specific organization like the NFPC confers authority or the lawful right to act.

The type of authority that the NFPC exercises is based on the moral involvement of the constituents. In other words, the NFPC exercises its authority as a moral influence rather than through coercion or holding out some utilitarian reward. This influence is based on the amount of commitment to and identification with the NFPC by the affiliates. It was shown in a portion of this chapter that the NFPC has gained a high degree of allegiance and identification from its participants as well as consensus about its structure of authority (refer to Table 5.1). It is clear that an overwhelming majority of the respondents accept the leadership's authority despite some dissent among the 1972 AM.

THE INFLUENCE OF THE NFPC

The evidence in Table 5.2 points to a growing influence of the NFPC on outside groups. The delegates feel that the NFPC's influence has not been substantial with the local bishop and the NCCB, but has considerable influence on the local councils, especially the associations.

The SM, compared to AM, give higher marks to the NFPC regarding its growth of influence on their bishops. An explanation of this paradoxical situation lies perhaps with this question of legitimacy. The senates are officially approved diocesan structures while almost all the associations are not. It is reasonable to assume that the NFPC's activities have become more acceptable in those dioceses in which such activities are linked with approved councils. Thus, after four years of existence, the NFPC has stabilized itself and is beginning to have some impact on the bishops.

In what areas has the NFPC exerted the most influence on the local councils? The evidence in Table 5.3 shows that the NFPC has considerable influence on the issues of handling priests' complaints and due process, some influence on social action programs, but little influence on the structural qualities of the local councils. It is reasonable to assume that the local diocesan priests and bishop would be more determinative of the local structure than the NFPC.

The NFPC has its greatest influence with the council affiliates on the issues of priests' rights and due process. The major hurdle with the bishops, however, is NFPC's lack of legitimacy. Based on available evidence, official approval will not be forthcoming for years to come if ever. Its influence with the bishops has been strengthened, however, by pragmatic efforts and programs which demonstrate to the bishops that the NFPC is not a threat to their authority.

Table 5.4 demonstrates that the officers and board of directors have the most influence on the NFPC's policies, followed by the delegates, the provincial units, and lastly local councils. The findings point to some type of elite influence, but is this really the case?

The literature on voluntary associations stresses democratic values of such organizations. There is an expectation that members will actively participate in the affairs of the organization and democratic processes will govern its conduct. But research also shows that, despite an organization's constitution and bylaws calling for such participation, there often arises a minority rule or the 'iron law of oligarchy'. Some factors contributing to this minority rule are the large number and heterogeneity of members, need for expertise, availability of time, and organizational specialization. Is the NFPC

Table 5.3   *Evaluation of NFPC's influence on local councils by council members (reported by percentages)**

	1969			1972			
	TOTAL delegates (N=203)	Senators (N=169)	Association members (N=30)	TOTAL delegates (N=186)	Senators (N=140)	Association members (N=34)	VARIATION of TM
Handling complaints of the councils	81	80	87	73	71	83	-8
Due process structures	74	72	87	61	57	77	-13
Launching social action programs	33	32	35	34	36	31	1
Revision of Constitution	20	20	17	10	7	23	-10
Change from advisory to legislative powers	4	4	3	1	1	0	-3

* Percentages represent only the positive evaluations. The negative evaluations of the delegates are not presented for the purpose of clarity.

Table 5.4 Evaluation of those groups having influence on the NFPC by council members (reported by percentages)*

	1969			1972			
	TOTAL delegates (N=203)	Senators (N=169)	Association members (N=30)	TOTAL delegates (N=186)	Senators (N=140)	Association members (N=34)	VARIATION OF TM
Officers and							
Executive Board	95	94	97	94	94	96	−1
House of Delegates	75	73	94	81	79	91	6
Provincial structure	34	33	48	39	41	37	5
Local councils	—	—	—	23	20	34	—

* Percentages represent only the positive evaluations. The negative evaluations of the delegates are not presented for the purpose of clarity.

oligarchical in its rule? Although it is clear from the above table that influence is structured at the top, it is located within units rather than individuals. Minority rule means that the same few individuals rule the organization over long periods of time. This type of rule is evident in many business and labor associations. But there are exceptions to the 'iron law of oligarchy'.

The NFPC's leadership is subject to the turnover process which makes it difficult for individuals to have a permanent sway. The officers and Executive Board can serve a maximum of two terms. Delegates usually serve less than this. Moreover, the influence of the national leadership is primarily moral persuasion rather than an exercise of utilitarian rewards or coercive sanctions. As I will show later, there is also a high degree of input and participation in the NFPC, evidenced by its democratic procedures. It is clear that a vertical power structure does not necessitate a minority rule. A great deal depends on democratic participation and leadership accountability. The NFPC has a large measure of both.

Research points to democratic processes as necessary conditions for effective voluntary associations. This form of power favors the continued involvement of the lower membership. Moreover, voluntary associations must remain open to new ideas if the democratic ethos is to be maintained. This flexibility aids greatly in maintaining the participation of the members around new issues to which they can rally their efforts and influence. This is also an important preventive measure against oligarchical rule. The next two chapters will show that the NFPC has been quite open to new ideas and issues. This is the result of institutionalizing democratic procedures in its structure.

In summary, the influence of the NFPC on both local councils and bishops during this period has been growing even though gradually. The power structure of the NFPC is vertical, with a concentration at the top. However, minority rule is checked both by constitutional provisions and by adequate democratic processes. I will now take up the question of how well the NFPC has been performing.

PERFORMANCE OF THE NFPC ·

A major focus for studying effectiveness is the analysis of organizational goals. One type of organizational effectiveness is defined in terms of goal achievement. I have pointed out, in my framework of effectiveness, that goal achievement is one of four prerequisites for organizational maintenance and survival.

The first task in assessing the goal effectiveness of the NFPC is goal identification. The criteria I use in this identification process is to examine what the major decision makers have to say about the goals of the NFPC. Then I locate the actual goals of the NFPC in contrast to the official goals or purposes found in its constitution. Finally, I assess what the leadership's orientations are, especially what they feel to be priority goals.

The reader will recall that 'value'-oriented persons expect rights and accept duties in generalized terms, independent of their particular relationship to the person himself or to this group affiliation. These persons are more concerned with social justice and commonweal goals. On the other hand, 'interest'-oriented persons are ones who are concerned about special rights and allocation of goods which the individuals or groups favor. In other words, they are interested in justice on a particularistic scale.

The NFPC goals which I have selected are meant to represent certain 'values' and 'interests' of the House of Delegates. I consider the following goals of the NFPC to be more 'value'-oriented, that is, to be desirable states that benefit the wider community rather than one's own status. These goals are (1) experimental ministries for a more relevant service to God's people and (2) social justice programs. The four 'interest' goals are (1) professional standards regulating priestly work, (2) changing the celibacy norm, (3) due process for the protection of priests' rights, and (4) a representative voice for priests regarding their concerns.

It is important to note that both 'value' and 'interest' goals may or may not be controversial. However, the most controversial goals are the 'interest' goals which impinge more directly on the authority of the bishops, especially in the area of clergy rights. Also, a specific goal may be controversial at one time but not at another time. One must also specify controversy in relationship to a concrete group.

Table 5.5 *Evaluation of the priority and effectiveness of operative goals of the NFPC by council members* (reported in percentages)†*

| | High priority | | | | | | Actually pursued | | | | | | Good progress | | | | | | Progress |
| | 1969 | | | 1972 | | | 1969 | | | 1972 | | | 1969 | | | 1972 | | | VARIATION |
	TM	SM	AM	TM	SM	AM	TM	SM	AM	TM	SM	AM	TM	SM	AM	TM	SM	AM	OF TM
INTEREST GOALS																			
Due process	86	86	90	94	92	100	95	94	100	90	90	91	78	79	78	80	84	69	2
Representative voice	80	77	93	93	92	97	91	90	93	86	84	94	67	65	72	71	72	66	3
Professional standards	65	64	70	91	92	85	78	77	76	72	71	76	21	20	23	39	56	52	18
Celibacy norm	54	50	76	80	81	74	71	69	84	75	74	79	25	23	25	35	36	31	10
VALUE GOALS																			
Social action programs	68	60	80	92	89	100	68	69	64	82	83	74	30	30	33	50	46	65	20
Experimental ministries	56	53	70	92	93	91	60	57	78	80	79	79	13	11	21	46	47	42	33

* The N for 1969 Delegates is TM(203), SM(169), AM(30); for 1972 TM(186), SM(140), AM(34). Religious Order representatives are not included in this analysis.

† Percentages represent only the positive evaluations. The negative evaluations of the delegates are not presented for the purpose of clarity.

My concept of controversy refers to issues which either attack or threaten episcopal authority and church discipline. Certainly the NFPC itself, as an organized response of the clergy to speak collectively, has been controversial to the bishops. The fact that the NCCB has never legitimated the NFPC is sufficient evidence. Other controversial issues, such as celibacy, have the lowest priority set by the delegates. Moreover, the goals of due process, experimental ministries, social action programs, and professionalization have ceased to be the major threats to episcopal authority they once were.

This list of goals is not exhaustive of the NFPC's objectives and programs, but it is representative of 'value' and 'interest' orientations. Table 5.5 below provides data on the priority and progress of the actual goals of the NFPC. From inspecting the data, especially the 1972 columns, one discovers a general pattern in which higher priority goals are those perceived to be the actual goals. They also register the most progress or effectiveness in absolute terms.

When one looks at the progress over time, goal effectiveness varies. The two highest priority goals of 1969 and 1972 register less effectiveness. Although this is perhaps due to the fact that these are the closest to attainment, it is also an indication of the NFPC's shift from 'interest' to 'value' goals. The lowest two priority goals, which are also 'interest' goals, show some progress over time. In absolute terms, however, they register the least amount of progress compared to the other goals. The reason for this is probably due to the controversy surrounding them. Both of these 'interest' goals threaten the bishops' authority over the life and work of priests. Development of professional standards would give priests more autonomy; optional celibacy would provide less regulation of one's personal life, such as place of residence, and a dramatic change in life style. A reason why some progress or effectiveness is registered in this area is due to the delegates' perception that the NFPC had put on a *tour de force* at the 1971 Baltimore convention. This will be discussed in detail in the next chapter.

The NFPC shows most progress in attaining the 'value' goals of the social ministry and the modernization of the pastoral ministry. These goals relate exclusively to serving people. Compared to 'interest' goals, there are less restrictions in the organizational environment to impede progress in this direction. One sees less activity around issues that have created controversy with the episcopal authorities and more activity regarding new policy directives in the area of pastoral and social ministry.

This points to the problem of how external constraints affect the progress of an organization relative to goals that are not within the spectrum of its influence. An organization may be effective in reaching its procurement, consolidation, and internal power objectives, but less effective in attaining those goals which are controlled by another group, in this case, the bishops. Such goals will be reached only when existing power arrangements are changed. But this will take some doing. The NFPC has recognized this and has begun to change its own emphasis toward programs outside the direct influence of the bishops, primarily in the social justice field.

In analyzing the goal priority dimension, one sees that the AM69 and AM72 are generally more 'value'-oriented than both SM groups. The SM increasingly have become more 'interest'-oriented. Refer especially to the last two 'interest' goals for 1972 in Table 5.5.

The AM69 are more optimistic about the NFPC progress than the SM69. But, paradoxically, the SM72 see more progress in goal effectiveness over this four year period than the AM72. As was noted earlier, the AM72 seem to be more impatient and alienated than the SM72. They have greater expectations at a time when the NFPC has slowed down from its exciting pace of 1968–1972 and has begun to shift to new and less controversial directions. Although the NFPC reorganized and expanded the Justice and Peace Committee, much to the liking of the AM72, it also started in 1972 to shift its concerns away from bishop-clergy power relationships to concrete ministerial concerns. As one delegate from the West Coast said: 'In Denver [1972 convention], there wasn't the storm as there was in last year's meeting in Baltimore. Denver got down to a lot of routine matters'.

What explains goal effectiveness is partially related to the intentions and activities of the leadership. If the leadership places higher priority on some goals than on others, then, barring outside restraints, one would expect more effort and probably more progress toward the realization of the priority goals. The findings in Table 5.6 point both to this relationship and to the limiting

Table 5.6   *Relationships between priority of goals and goal effectiveness**

	Priority of the goal	
	1969	1972
PROGRESS OF		
Becoming a representative voice	.337	.854
Developing experimental ministries	.206	.469
Launching social action programs	.193	.441
Developing structures of due process	.122	.382
Developing professional standards	−.124	−.028
Launching discussions on celibacy	−.213	−.163

* Gamma coefficients. A coefficient of 1.00 would signify a perfect association or 'cause' between priority and progress.

conditions of the external environment.

From the 1969 data it is evident that there is little relationship between priority and goal effectiveness. It is the story of high expectations not automatically translating into realizations. In 1969, the NFPC was both young and aggressive and above all autonomous from the bishops' control. Their demands for changes in the priestly life, role, and ministry were a threat to episcopal power. The climate in the church at that time militated against the achievement of goals felt to be within the province of the bishops. The only organizational goal over which they had complete control was that of developing a representative voice. It was on this goal that priority and progress had their strongest relationship in both 1969 and 1972.

There is a pattern between priority and effectiveness in the 1972 data. The higher the priority assigned to a goal, the greater the progress or effectiveness toward reaching that goal. The due process goal seems to be an exception to this pattern. The relationship of

priority and progress is the strongest on the first three goals cited in
Table 5.6. Regarding the due process, the NFPC faced a great
deal of opposition by the bishops because of its independence and
militancy during the years between 1969 and 1972. Thus, the
opposition factor of the bishops weakens the priority and progress
relationship. The negative relationships between priority and progress of the last two 'interest'-oriented goals can also be explained
by the continued hostility of the bishops. The lesser the external
opposition, the stronger the relationship of goal effectiveness and
the priority intentions of the leadership. Another way of putting it,
the NFPC and priests in general are powerless against the bishops
on issues where their opposition is strong, united, and unyielding.
One such issue area is the various aspects of secual morality.

In sum, the NFPC is becoming more 'value'-oriented in its
emphasis, moving away from 'interests' issues which promote
bishop-priests entanglements. The respondents thus evaluate the
NFPC more effective on the 'value' goals than on the 'interest'
goals.

During ensuing years the NFPC has continued a policy of
non-confrontation with the bishops by setting priorities in the area
of ministry and social justice. For instance, the agendas for the
Detroit (1973), San Francisco (1974), and St. Petersburg (1975)
meetings confirm this shift. I call this strategy pragmatic militancy
for social justice. It is a policy that says that there's more than
enough work for renewing the pastoral ministry both spiritually and
socially. The NFPC as an autonomous group, can make a contribution to society without episcopal endorsement. Thus, it is a policy
that says: move forward with or without episcopal support; declare
loyalty and cooperation with the bishops, but move forcefully into
important areas of societal concern which don't impinge on episcopal authority.

It is this genius of serving multiple goals and satisfying diverse
orientations which makes the NFPC both stable and flexible, having
the structural capacity to renew and balance itself in a continuous
manner. It would be a disaster to organizational democracy for one
or the other type of council to disaffiliate. The challenge to the
NFPC is to improve itself as an effective tool for greater service; yet,
to be always on guard that the tool doesn't become the master

wherein the power to influence lies in the hands of the few. I will now turn to a more historical account of the changing directions, purposes, and activities of the NFPC since its founding to the beginning of 1976.

6

Priests' Interests:
A Period of Confrontation,
1968–1972

INTRODUCTION

The NFPC was founded to mobilize local priests' councils in an effort to improve the quality of the clergy and speed the pace of reform in the church and society. The Federation signified the continuing demands by priests for more say within the church. Initially the Federation would deal with limited areas, such as career expectations, professional status, personnel questions, restrictions on personal freedom, and co-responsibility.

Uppermost in the minds of these priests was the crisis in the church resulting from changes wrought by Vatican II. Priests agonized over the problems of renewing the faith and ministry; collegiality; restrictions of priests' rights of conscience, speech, and assembly; leadership gaps; and the definition of the priest. The Federation had an immediate problem of legitimatizing itself to both the rank-and-file priests and the bishops. The president of the NFPC, Father O'Malley, said that the NFPC has a right to exist; it is within the spirit of Vatican II in the democratic sense of collegiality. He went on to say: 'The bishop is no longer king. We don't have to ask permission to undertake our [NFPC] projects' (*Time*, 1968). The tone was set. The NFPC was saying in effect that priests weren't hired hands but were partners with the bishops in the ministry. They expected and were to demand respect as professionals. Almost immediately the NFPC was embroiled in the controversy of due process with Cardinal O'Boyle. They bargained for the rights of priests. The leaders of the NFPC felt that the Council had let them down. They were the ones who were at the forefront of the ministry; yet they were being treated as second-class citizens. They were not anarchists, but serious professionals. While respecting their superiors, they would confront them with their injustices.

With the founding of the NFPC, democracy entered the priesthood. The organization expended a great deal of energy to insure that the issues of the grassroots were heard. The business of the Federation was simply communication and representation. Through a series of twenty provincial meetings, topics were developed ranging from relations with the bishops and reform of canon law to social action and spirituality. These would constitute the agenda of the New Orleans meeting in 1969. One problem which did command much of the NFPC's attention and action was the issue of due process mentioned above. In response to the situation that had arisen in Washington, D.C., and San Antonio, the Executive Board determined that the theme for the 1969 meeting would be due process and collegiality (Executive Board Minutes, 1968).

One of the NFPC's top priorities was to establish an effective liaison with the bishops through the NCCB. In the fall of 1968, the Executive Board had several meetings with Cardinal Shehan to explain the purpose of the NFPC and to affirm the desire for a collegial relationship with the hierarchy. Finally, the Executive Board met in November with the NCCB Liaison Committee for the purpose of discussing the due process issue and to further talks about the kinds of relationships that might be possible between the two groups. The NFPC also petitioned to be heard at the November meeting of the NCCB, but was denied (President's Newsletter, 1968). This reaction hardened the relationship for some time to come. The primary emphasis and direction of the NFPC concerned priests' interests in terms of sharing in the decision making of the hierarchy, priests' rights, and personnel policies. This emphasis, together with a militant approach, would continue through the Baltimore convention in 1971.

NEW ORLEANS 1969: FREEDOM AND PRIESTS' RIGHTS

The stock joke in priests' circles concerning the rights of an assistant pastor is that the priest has one basic right: that of Christian burial. But the rights of priests were a serious concern to the 230 delegates at this convention. At the opening session, Father O'Donoghue, one of the Washington, D.C., suspended priests, had moved that the planned agenda of speeches and discussion of internal Church affairs be scrapped in favor of open debate on the Vatican stand on birth control, world peace, and racial and poverty programs (Herman, 1969: 1). His motion was rejected. The delegates were determined to tackle what they considered the most necessary issues, if not the most important—freedom of priests and participation in the power structure. If the obstacles to these interests weren't removed, no amount of effort could solve the problems of the commonweal. Sharing the power was the guiding motif of the convention. To the NFPC, power meant a common voice, a coalesced energy, a unified initiative—not to force or coerce the bishops, but to cooperate with them in carrying out the renewal. Cardinal Shehan, speaking for himself, echoed this sentiment when he stated that he was speaking to the delegates as 'a fellow priest who happens to be the archbishop of Baltimore' (Sigur, 1969: 1).

In his address to the Federation, Father O'Malley emphasized this need for collegiality and collaboration; but with this was the need for professional autonomy, rights of priests, due process, and the democratic process within the Church. Throughout the speech was the spirit of freedom, with specific references to the revision of canon law, selection of bishops, priests' life style, experimentation in the ministry, social action initiatives, and optional celibacy (O'Malley, 1969b).

Some, like Father O'Donoghue, felt that too much attention was to be devoted to the internal affairs of the priesthood, such as personnel matters and organizational guidelines for local councils. Because of his influence the regular agenda was shortened, leaving the last day for discussions on social justice and peace issues. And though crucial societal issues received attention, they were of secondary importance to the NFPC at this convention (*National Catholic Reporter*, 1969a).

Resolutions

There were thirty-two resolutions passed at this convention. Eight involved social action (justice and peace) issues, eleven were on the ministry and priestly life, eight involved personnel matters, two were on priests' councils and laity, and three dealt with the internal affairs of the NFPC. (Refer to the end of this chapter for a comparative analysis of these resolutions and those that were passed in the following two years.)

Most of the resolutions, eighteen in all, dealt with 'interest' issues. As shown elsewhere, 'interests' are related to power relations. They deal with rights and prerogatives attached to the status of an individual or group. 'Value'-oriented persons or groups stir people to break away from the status quo to bring about a greater social good. See Sr. Augusta Neal (1965) for a further elaboration.

Although the NFPC was concerned with 'value' questions, the main emphasis was with these 'interest' issues. The issue that occupied most of the delegates' attention was due process, which took the form of the following resolution. The resolution contained three points (Proceedings, 1969: 32):

1. The NFPC called on the National Conference of Catholic Bishops to appoint a fact-finding committee to resolve the San Antonio and Washington disputes.
2. If the conference does not, the NFPC itself will appoint a committee to take appropriate action.
3. Until due process is a functioning reality in the church, the NFPC will offer its services to appoint fact-finding boards to mediate similar disputes when no reasonable resolution is possible through ordinary channels.

The resolutions expressed the concern of the delegates for the individual priests involved in the disputes. One of the spokesmen, Father Bill Murphy of Detroit, said that one action might be for the NFPC to hire civil and canon lawyers to press civil rights suits in secular courts or to take an appeal directly to Rome (*New Orleans States-Item*, 1969: 1).

Other 'interest' resolutions dealt with personnel accountability and evaluation, priests' life style, reform of canon law, laicization, optional celibacy, council structures, and the position and relationships of bishops. This last area had six resolutions dealing with various aspects of collegiality. The 'value' resolutions on social action and experimental ministries were not as strongly worded as the 'interest' resolutions.

It was clear from the very outset that the 'interests' of the priests would command the greatest priority and attention of the delegates. They rejected the charge that the prepared agenda was irrelevant.

The last day was rescheduled to reserve time for discussing these wider 'value' questions. As an observer at this meeting, it was obvious to me that these Wednesday discussions turned out to be dismal failures. The leadership of the NFPC felt, and probably rightly so, that it must pay urgent attention to those concerns that touch the priesthood directly before moving on to issues of the common good; otherwise, priests' rights and powers might continue to be ignored. Above all, the New Orleans meeting was a call to action.

In sum, the NFPC initiated a policy that dealt with the 'interest' issues of the priests. Collegiality, due process, and professional standards were their main concern. Priests were fighting for a meaningful place in the Church. The NFPC articulated these desires. The tone was one of action, even of confrontation if necessary. As one priest-delegate said, in effect: if the NFPC has to die in the fight for priests' right, it's a fight worth dying for (*New Orleans States-Item*, 1969: 6).

THE AFTERMATH: 1969–1970

As might be expected, due process and the Washington 19 remained the most crucial of NFPC issues. During the Executive Board meeting immediately following the convention it was determined that, if the NCCB took no action, the NFPC would provide for the preparation of the cases of the Washington, D.C., and San Antonio priests for presentation to Rome. Further, if no action was taken by Rome after three months, a special meeting of the House of Delegates would be called (Executive Board Minutes, 1969: 3). On May 7, 1969, the National Catholic Reporter (1969b) announced that the Executive Board had voted to take the cases of the Washington 19 to official Church courts in Rome, as the NCCB had failed to respond to its request.

Throughout 1969, then, the NFPC's major concerns were due process and shared responsibility. In preparing these cases, the NFPC emphasized that its actions involved neither the substance of the *Humanae Vitae* nor the legitimacy of ecclesiastical authority, but the issue of protecting priests' rights (*Priests' Forum*, 1969a).

The tribunals of Washington and Cleveland rejected the petitions of the Washington 19. Finally, the NFPC and the Committee of Concerned Canon Lawyers petitioned directly to Rome for a review of the case.

Father O'Malley set the tone for the NFPC's stand on shared responsibility in a discussion of the Synod of Bishops' October meeting. He stated that the NFPC must be an instrument for systematic change within the Church and, as such, its top priority must be the sharing of decision making. With this in mind, he emphasized the need for structural links with the NCCB, democratic selection and limited tenure of bishops, and the need for effective leadership (O'Malley, 1969a).

Other resolutions were being implemented by the respective standing committees. Continuing Education was researching what types of educational programs were available to priests in the dioceses. The Role of the Priest Committee worked on researching new approaches to problems of priests. The Priests' Councils and Laity Committee worked on developing models to examine the effectiveness of local councils. The Personnel Committee sponsored a workshop on personnel procedures and professional standards. The Social Action Committee worked on educating the councils on social justice issues. The Research Committee began working on a national study of celibacy and stress under the direction of John Koval and Richard Bell. Provincial meetings were held again in the fall to gather information on topics of needs of and services to the priesthood, which were to constitute the agenda for the next convention. The NFPC was encouraged by the attendance of non-affiliated councils, as well as of a number of bishops. The emphasis of these activities throughout the year was clearly directed to the 'interest' issues of the priests.

THE BISHOPS AND THE NFPC

The NFPC sent letters to Archbishop Dearden, the president of the NCCB, and all the bishops, informing them of the House of Delegates' resolutions regarding due process. The delegates were asked to contact their respective ordinaries for the purpose of informing them of the local council's stand on due process and to request representation at the NCCB's national meetings. On April 13, 1969, the NFPC officers met with the Bishops' Liaison Committee, requesting that the bishops take action on the due process resolutions; but no action was taken on these issues by the bishops at their April 16 meeting in Houston. Furthermore, the situations at Washington, D.C., and San Antonio were not discussed (Memorandum, 1969: 1).

While much of the NFPC-NCCB interaction was essentially an attempt by the NFPC to initiate NCCB action regarding the issues of due process, the NFPC's primary concern was to gain recognition from the NCCB in order to achieve some sense of understanding and collaboration between the two organizations. Father O'Malley reported a 'most positive' meeting with Archbishop McDonough and the Liaison Committee, in which he discussed some of the bishops' misgivings about the NFPC and attempted to dispel the notion that the NFPC is a pressure group (*National Catholic Reporter*, 1969c). To achieve this clarification with the NCCB, the NFPC requested that Father O'Malley be given the opportunity to address the NCCB at the Houston meeting. The request was refused on the basis that there was no precedent for any outsider to address the bishops' assembly. Yet it was subsequently learned that three 'outsiders' did address the meeting (*Priests' Forum*, 1969b).

Further contact with the NCCB was made in June when the NFPC sent a document containing the theological rationale for the NFPC to the NCCB Doctrinal Committee. In September, the NFPC polled all the councils for proposed topics for discussion at the forthcoming Synod of Bishops in Rome. The results were forwarded to Archbishop Dearden as NFPC recommendations (*Priests' Forum*, 1969c: 2).

On October 16, the NFPC officers again met with the Bishops' Liaison Committee in hopes of making some progress toward greater sharing of decision making. Specifically, the NFPC again requested that its president be allowed to address the NCCB's November meeting and that each ordinary be accompanied at the spring, 1970, meeting of the NCCB by the president of the local senate or an elected delegate (*Priests' Forum*, 1969b).

Although this latter request was rejected, O'Malley did address the November NCCB meeting, calling for collaboration between the two groups on areas of concern to the Church; recognition by the NCCB that it needs the NFPC; and the development of a national policy-making board which would involve priests, religious, and laity with the hierarchy (O'Malley, 1969c).

While little headway was being made on the national level between the NFPC and NCCB during this year, much more communication and cooperation was in evidence at the provincial meetings.

THE NFPC AND LOCAL COUNCILS

During this period many local councils were restructuring themselves. Some were having difficulties with their bishops. The senates of Yakima, Washington, and Crookston, Minnesota, resigned en masse because the senate and the bishop were not able to work together successfully. Senates and associations reported the following problems facing their councils: (1) apathy of the priests in general, (2) lack of cooperation from the bishops, and (3) failure to resolve the problem of whether a council is merely represenative and consultative or should exert leadership (*NFPC Newsletter*, 1968b: 3). In those dioceses where the senates weren't functioning well, many associations were formed and affiliated with the NFPC. The number of NFPC affiliates grew from 114 in May, 1968, to 134 by June, 1969. During this period, the NFPC changed its Executive Board membership from twenty-nine to twenty-seven members, representing the twenty-seven provinces of the country. The positions of religious orders and the Eastern Catholic community were dropped. The Social Action Committee's name was changed to Human Resources and Development.

It was shown in the last two chapters that the 1969 delegates were in high agreement with the NFPC's work and goals. There was a great deal of cohesion and morale among these leaders. However, a great deal of effort was needed to integrate the NFPC into an effective, communicative, and collaborative organization. Its influence on the local councils was significant, but left much to be done. Its influence on the local bishop was modest, and regarding the rank and file its influence was almost nil. The incipient provincial structures were viewed as potentially the most effective instrument to implement the NFPC's policies.

SAN DIEGO 1970: SHARED RESPONSIBILITY

Over 250 delegates, representing 130 affiliated councils, came to San Diego to deliberate the crucial issue of co-responsibility. While the delegates were neither raucous nor radical, the tone was nevertheless serious and impatient, although tempered by the respect given to the five bishops present.

An important feature of the meeting was its openness. Reporters remarked about the complete availability of the leaders and about the open sessions. This was in marked contrast to the closed nature of the bishops' meetings. The NFPC understood the importance of bringing public opinion to bear on the decision makers (Dollen, 1970: 62–63). When the convention ended, the NFPC had a new president, Father Frank Bonnike of DeKalb, Illinois. Father Bonnike had been associated with the NFPC since its inception and had worked on the due process issue of the Washington 19 case.

In a keynote address, Bishop Alexander Carter (Carter, 1970: 12–13), president of the Canadian Catholic Conference, said:

You carry a terrible responsibility. The influence of your country is perhaps greater than you yourselves realize. The love-hate complex which seems at times to mark bishop-priests relations in your Church is somewhat similar to the love-hate affair that underlies apparent antagonism towards America in so many parts of the world. We pray for the Church of the United States. It will be a tragedy of cosmic dimension if the confrontations there erupt into division and shatter the basic unity and cohesion of the Church in America.

Father O'Malley (O'Malley, 1970: 15–17) addressed the delegates with no holds barred. He said: 'Our potential for preaching the good news of Christ—of freedom and responsibility—is limited not so much by the system but by our unwillingness to tackle the system and make it work to free men'. He went on to say 'that the institutionalized Church can be an instrument by which we are used, becoming nothing more than obedient automatons afraid to face the challenge to which the Son of Man has called us. We make that choice ourselves. We will push for shared responsibility because it is essential to the life of the Church'.

Father O'Malley's address on the 'State of the Federation' was essentially the same one that he delivered to the NCCB meeting in November, 1969. Explaining the major purpose of the NFPC in terms of across-the-board cooperation and collaboration between priests, laity, and the hierarchy on every level, he cited the momentum of frustration developing among the priests and laity. The tone of the speech was basically one of respectful confrontation, but confrontation nonetheless. He outlined three steps necessary to strengthen hope in the priests and in the church at large: (1) the NFPC and NCCB must work together on important issues, such as continuing education, personnel affairs, priestly spirituality, pastoral councils, and due process; (2) the NCCB must admit openly and effectively that it needs the NFPC; and (3) the NFPC and the NCCB must work to develop a national pastoral council. He also cited other internal problems of the Church, such as solutions to the problem of mandatory celibacy, change in the laicization procedures, selection and accountability of leadership, reform of canon law, and inter-cooperation among Church organizations. The third session was devoted to this last issue of organizational cooperation. Representatives from six lay, religious, and clergy organizations discussed ways of cooperating with the NFPC. The remainder of the convention dealt with committee reports and resolutions.

The policies of the NFPC continued to emphasize the 'interest' issues of the priest, especially the area of co-responsibility in decision making. The NFPC was talking tougher. The approach was increasingly militant and confrontative (see *National Catholic Reporter*, 1970a; *America*, 1970; and *Christianity Today*, 1970).

Resolutions

There were forty-eight resolutions passed at the San Diego meeting. There were thirteen dealing with the ministry and priestly life; fourteen regarding personnel questions; four dealing with priests' councils and laity; three regarding continuing education; four related to social justice; and the remaining ten dealt with internal affairs. Thirty resolutions were 'interest' resolutions dealing with normative concerns of priests, personnel affairs, bishop-clergy relationships of power, priests' and pastoral councils, and continuing education. Eight resolutions were 'value'-oriented, dealing with experimental and specialized ministries to homosexuals and with social justice issues. It is clear that the NFPC was continuing its policy emphasis in the direction of priests' 'interests'. Refer to the end of the chapter for a description of these resolutions.

There were five 'interest' resolutions dealing with due process and four dealing with the question of optional celibacy. Seven resolutions dealt with personnel accountability and evaluation and three concerned the continuing education of priests. Three others regarded shared responsibility through the enactment of diocesan and national pastoral councils. Finally, eight resolutions dealt with the issue of co-responsibility with the bishops.

Continuing education of priests was given a top priority, and the committee urged that a House of Prayer and Study be established in every diocese. The Personnel Committee's resolutions covered in detail the issues of recruitment, training, forms of ministry, retirement, due process boards, salaries, rectory relationships, and the recommendation that assistant pastors be given some pastoral rights (Dollen, 1970: 62–63). However, the greatest attention was devoted to the NFPC-NCCB relationships and the due process issues.

The convention was a call to action. Born out of a situation of powerlessness, nurtured by militancy, and tempered by professional respect for one's superiors, the NFPC sowed the new seeds of hope for the church. One reporter (Dollen, 1970: 64) put it this way:

NFPC itself learned a much needed lesson in that it must take greater strides to implement its decisions. If the bishops of our country will enter into honest dialogue with NFPC, a new day will dawn for our Church. . . .

PROGRESS AFTER THE SAN DIEGO CONVENTION

The San Diego convention had voted to cable the Holy Father to grant a petition for an impartial hearing for the Washington 19. It further voted to hold a special meeting of the House of Delegates on April 20 if no action had been taken by then. Father Bonnike stressed that the April 20 deadline was not to force the Pope, but rather was to allow time for the NFPC to decide what alternative actions might be taken. Suggestions ranged from a day of prayer to some form of a strike (Olmstead, 1970). The April 20 meeting was cancelled when, on April 18, a letter from the Apostolic Delegate announced that a reply to the NFPC's letter would be forthcoming (*National Catholic Reporter*, 1970b). By August 13, the case was before the Sacred Congregation of the Clergy in Rome. Nothing was heard of the case until March, 1971. *Priests-USA* (1971a), the new journal of the NFPC, reported that 'after two and one-half years the priests . . . are receiving an impartial hearing which they, along with the committee of Concerned Canon Lawyers and the NFPC, have been seeking'.

In the interest of strengthening the NFPC's work in the areas of social action, the Executive Board hired two part-time staff, Fathers Gene Boyle and Bob Kennedy, to work with the Human Resources and Development Committee (later called Justice and Peace). On the initiative of Boyle, the December Executive Board telegrammed the lettuce growers, urging them to accept the California clergymen as mediators (Executive Board Minutes, 1970b: 5).

Another area of concern to the NFPC at this time was the notion of a National Pastoral Council. Yet the National Advisory Council of the USCC had serious questions about the feasibility of such a council. It felt a more fruitful approach would be regional developments. From August 28 to 30, an open forum on the feasibility of a National Pastoral Council was sponsored by the NAC. The NFPC participated in the meeting and the NAC resolved to compile a booklet on these deliberations, secure grassroots reactions, and make a final presentation of the feasibility of such a council by September, 1971. The NFPC commissioned a special issue of *Chicago Studies* for September, 1970, to address the entire area of shared responsibility and pastoral councils (Executive Board Minutes, 1970a: 3).

Other efforts were directed to continuing education workshops, spiritual life symposia, and the development of 'Priests' Personnel Documentary Service'.

The NFPC and the NCCB

Father Bonnike presented seventeen topics for discussion at the August meeting of the NCCB's Liaison Committee. All but three of the issues concerned 'interest' concerns of the NFPC. In particular, Bonnike suggested that the NCCB and the NFPC should work together following the completion of the studies on the priesthood and celibacy. Bishop Bernardin said that the NCCB study 'stands on its own' and asked if the NFPC study was done because of suspicion of the NCCB. Father Graney of the NFPC staff said that there was no suspicion regarding the competence or honesty of the study, but only suspicion that the findings would be kept secret or only reported in part. The NFPC requested the release of the raw data, but this was denied (NFPC-NCCB Liaison Committee Meeting, 1970: 5).

Also during this period, the NFPC urged priest representation at the World Synod of Bishops and requested that the bishops of each region convoke an annual meeting of bishops and clergy to discuss the NCCB's agenda. The NCCB did decide to hold diocesan and provincial meetings with priests, religious, and laity to evaluate the NFPC's proposal and to prepare for the World Synod (Bonnike, 1970).

The NFPC took the initiative in attempting cooperation with the bishops through the NCCB. The NCCB's reaction during this year was a mixture of vacillation, suspicion, and begrudging cooperation. The relationship evidenced the love-hate syndrome referred to by Bishop Carter at the San Diego convention. If the interaction between the NFPC and the NCCB was now marked by tension, the relationship would become hardened and confrontative after the Baltimore meeting.

Baltimore 1971: The Moment of Truth

The NFPC was becoming a force with which to reckon. It had helped to win a fair hearing of the Washington 19. It was the only autonomous, deliberative, and representative body of priests in the world at that time. Many bishops, priests, and laity still expressed fears about the NFPC's 'power and disloyalty'. The NFPC had dug its way into the still-under-construction area of shared responsibility—a principle that the bishops, during Vatican II, had agreed to implement. Since its founding, the NFPC had won a grudging acknowledgment of its existence from the hierarchy (Haughey, 1971: 341). In Baltimore, from March 14 to 18, 235 delegates and alternates, representing 132 affiliates, debated the key issue of the convention: optional celibacy. The resolution, adopted by a roll call vote—an unusual procedure—of 182 to 23, urgently requested from the bishops of the world a plan for the immediate change in the disciplinary laws leading to optional celibacy. The actual words of the resolution were: 'We ask that the choice between celibacy and marriage for priests now active in the ministry be allowed and that the change begin immediately' (*Priests-USA*, 1971c: 5).

Why such a radical decision? Several factors leading to this resolution were influential. One was the fact that the delegates had previously surveyed the climate of their councils before coming to the convention. All the councils had received a draft of the 'Moment of Truth' statement prior to the convention. The overwhelming vote for the resolution by the delegate-represenatives presumably manifested the general sentiment of the rank and file. The NFPC also had the results of their study on celibacy (Koval and Bell, 1971). The findings showed that 73% of a national sample of priests favored ordination of married men. The study also reported that 56% of the priests favored optional celibacy for priests now active in the ministry, with 36% saying that they would consider marriage if the law changed. Lastly, the delegates were informed by Father Eugene Schallert that 25,000 priests had resigned in the past seven years (Haughey, 1971: 341).

The final text of the 'Moment of Truth' statement was brief and to the point. Father Bonnike, the president of the NFPC, told the delegates that it was to be a 'political' document aimed at the bishops and the Synod. The emotion and tone of the convention was centered on this issue. One of the significant things about the entire debate was that the question never became one of whether or why, but only of how and when, the relaxation of the present discipline should take place (Haughey, 1971: 342).

The proceedings also included a series of resolutions related to the military and the war in Southeast Asia. There were unanimous votes backing the United Farm Workers; the National Office of Black Catholics; and Project Amos, which conerned the plight of day laborers.

The mood of the convention was one of steadfastness and boldness. They felt that change in the Church was not a result of some blind uncontrollable force, but was in the hands of those courageous enough to take leadership. Monsignor John Egan (Egan, 1971: 102) put it this way:

They crave intelligent and shared leadership from their superiors, but, in its absence, refuse to allow the vacuum of leadership to daunt them any longer . . . [but] to manfully assume leadership, to speak and act boldly in the building of the Kingdom of God.

Many of the 'interest' issues which had been developed in New Orleans and San Diego reached a climax at the Baltimore convention. The House of Delegates, with an eye to the Synod of Bishops meeting in Rome in October, forged a statement which addressed the crucial internal problems of Church structure, leadership, rights of due process, priestly renewal, and celibacy. While celibacy was the most burning issue, the delegates identified the lack of leadership as the major problem confronting priests. The NFPC called for the implementation of the suggestions of the Canon Law Society for the selection of bishops. In addition, there was a demand for protection of human rights within the Church, and the development of new forms of ministry. (See Appendix C for the complete text of the 'Moment of Truth' statement. This statement was the 'State of the Federation' address delivered by Father Bonnike.)

The policies and directions of the NFPC from its inception through the Baltimore convention and up to the Denver convention were aimed primarily at solving the 'interest' issues of priests. Priests' rights, shared power, and freedom in priests' life style were the dominant themes. The talk was tough, the approach militant, and the demands straightforward, if not confrontative. Paradoxically, there was a great respect for the bishops and the NCCB. But the NFPC leaders saw themselves as professional men and, as such, they were not going to tolerate being treated as lackeys.

Resolutions

There were thirty-one resolutions passed at the Baltimore convention. There were fifteen 'value' resolutions dealing with social action (Justice and Peace). Eight of these dealt with one area, the military and war. The other 'value' resolutions concerned experimental ministries. There were twelve 'interest' resolutions dealing with personnel affairs, bishop-clergy relations, and normative interests of priests. Quantitatively, if the eight resolutions on the military and war are considered as one, the 'interest' resolutions predominated at the meeting. But, in any regard, the intensity of the meeting and the saliency of issues concerned the 'interest' issues of the priests in the United States.

Inspecting Table 6.1 it is clear that, from its inception, the NFPC's policies were geared to the internal problems of the priesthood. Overall, there were sixty-one 'interest' resolutions dealing with normative interests of priests, such as due process, personnel affairs, bishop-clergy relations, priest' councils, and continuing education. One-half of these resolutions were passed at the San Diego convention. On the other hand, there were only thirty-four 'value' resolutions during this time, dealing with social justice and peace issues and the pastoral ministry. There wasn't a strong emphasis on social justice issues until Baltimore. Up to the Baltimore meeting there were only twelve resolutions dealing with the commonweal and six dealing with the pastoral ministry. Resolutions are carried out sometimes with great success like due process issue and the establishment of personnel boards, and sometimes with failure such as dialogue with the bishops concerning married priests. Some resolutions merely call for a statement from the NFPC such as condemning the Vietnam War. Others involve launching a national association such as the continuing education of clergy. While some resolutions are the responsibility of the national leadership or one of their task forces, many resolutions are implemented by the local councils. (See the summary table in Appendix IV for a comparative analysis of all the conventions' resolutions.)

The NFPC felt, and rightly so, that it had to pay attention to the area undeveloped by Vatican II. It also realized that the forces of the secular world were contributing to the loss of meaning and functions

Table 6.1 *Resolutions passed at NFPC Conventions, 1969–71*

	1969 (N = 32)	1970 (N = 48)	1971 (N = 31)	1969–71 (N = 111)
JUSTICE AND PEACE	*8*	*4*	*15*	*27*
1. Civil rights	1	0	1	2
2. Economic justice	3	3	4	10
3. War and peace	2	0	8	10
4. International justice	0	0	2	2
5. Polictical justice	0	0	0	0
6. Community organization and needs	2	1	0	3
MINISTRY AND PRIESTLY LIFE	*11*	*13*	*5*	*29*
1. Normative interests of priests	9	9	4	22
2. Ministerial concerns	0	3	0	3
3. Alternative ministries	2	1	1	4
PERSONNEL	*8*	*14*	*8*	*30*
1. Accountability and evaluation	1	6	4	11
2. Research and development on priest distribution	1	0	0	1
3. Bishop-clergy relations	6	8	4	18
COMMUNICATIONS	*0*	*1*	*0*	*1*
RESEARCH AND DEVELOPMENT	*0*	*0*	*0*	*0*
FINANCE	*2*	*2*	*3*	*7*
PRIEST'S COUNCILS AND LAITY	*2*	*4*	*0*	*6*
1. Pastoral councils	1	3	0	4
2. Evaluation	1	1	0	2
CONTINUING EDUCATION	*0*	*3*	*0*	*3*
CONSTITUTION AND INTERNAL AFFAIRS	*1*	*7*	*0*	*8*

of the priesthood. The Civil Rights Movement of the 1960s made it clear to the NFPC that priests, especially assistant pastors, had neither human nor professional rights in the Church. These problems were of urgent concern because priests were resigning and young men weren't entering the seminary. The NFPC responded to these crises of definition, rights, and powers with expertise and professionalism. Though criticized by the more liberal delegates, the leadership felt that it had to formulate policy and strategies to solve the internal problems of the priesthood before it could move on to wider 'value' concerns.

After Baltimore

Following the Baltimore meeting and the acceptance of the 'Moment of Truth' statement, the NFPC was charged with not being a representative organization. In June, 1971, two councils disaffiliated due to the Baltimore meeting. Father Bonnike responded to these charges, defending and explaining the concept of representative government (Bonnike, 1971a). In December, the Executive Board considered seven alternative structures for the NFPC, but decided to retain the existing one. However, constitutional provisions were proposed which would improve representation by allowing affiliation by supra-diocesan groups (Executive Board Minutes, 1971: 11).

By late summer one began to notice a transition in policy emphasis. In August, Father Bonnike suggested that the topic of top priority at the Synod meeting should be world justice rather than the priesthood. He hoped that the Synod would take up the topics of the specific duties of a Christian in opposing injustice and the causes of world injustice, as well as the issue of the married priesthood (Bonnike, 1971b). In January, 1972, the NFPC announced two important items that confirmed the transition from 'interest' emphasis to 'value' emphasis in policy direction. One was the announcement of hiring a full-time director of the Justice and Peace Committee; the other was the announcement of the theme for the forthcoming Denver convention: 'Ministry for Justice and Peace: Imperative for Priests-USA'. In essence, the policy and plans for the Denver meeting were to give substance to the directions given by the Third International Synod of Bishops (*Priests-USA*, 1972c).

THE NFPC AND THE BISHOPS

Much of the NFPC-NCCB interaction centered around the NFPC's attempt for greater priest representation both to the NCCB and the World Synod. The NCCB decided to hold regional meetings with priests, religious, and laity to prepare for their April meetings. Father Bonnike noted that, from the NFPC's viewpoint, the meetings were extremely disappointing (*Priests-USA*, 1971d). But the NFPC's request that priests be represented at the World Synod resulted in the appointment of two U.S. priests as observers at the Synod (*Priests-USA*, 1971b). The April meeting of the NCCB proved to be a big disappointment to the NFPC. The NFPC noted that little attempt was made toward improving relations between the two groups. Disappointment lay both with the NCCB's choice of conservative bishops as representatives to the Synod, and with the NCCB's failure to address the important issues contained in the "Moment of Truth" statement, as well as their attempt to dominate the lives of priests (*Priests-USA*, 1971e). *Newsweek* (1971a: 74) described the NCCB meeting in Detroit in the following way: '. . . [the bishops] spent much of their semiannual meeting in Detroit last week debating—and roundly criticizing—reports on the priesthood that they themselves had commissioned'.

Some of the bishops charged the NFPC as self-serving. Bonnike answered this charge by indicating the NCCB's own narrowness in its complete failure to listen to priests. He went on to ask who had assisted priests in developing new models of prayer, developed programs of continuing education, and helped personnel chairmen to relate to the problems cited by the Greeley and Kennedy studies. It hadn't been the NCCB. He also said that the NFPC was tired of being called divisive in its efforts to serve the Church. He warned the bishops that the military model must go (Bonnike, 1971c).

In August, Fathers Bonnike and Paul Boyle, head of the Leadership Conference of Religious Men, were selected as auditors to the World Synod. While in Rome, Bonnike stated that he found the bishops unwilling to deal realistically with those issues related to the shortage of priests, especially the issue of optional celibacy (McEoin, 1971).

Some progress in cooperation between the NFPC and the NCCB

was evident during the fall and winter. Some of the NFPC's requests conveyed to the NCCB were put on the fall agenda. In addition, the NCCB asked Father Bonnike to serve on its Committee on Implementing the Priesthood Studies (*Priests-USA*, 1972b).

Accompanying a gradual shift of emphasis to justice and peace issues was the beginning of a shift in attitude toward the bishops. Of the two major topics at the December Executive Board meeting, one recommended that the NFPC stop sparring with bishops. It asked that priests work toward building more accountability and trust between bishops and priests; it called upon priests to abandon inertia and prod their own consciences, and to aim for basic concurrence between themselves and the bishops (*Priests-USA*, 1972a: 1). Thus, the NFPC was approaching a new threshold. Though not abandoning the 'interest' issues that commanded their attention over the past three years, it would begin to emphasize the pastoral and social ministry—thus becoming more 'value'-oriented. What controversies the NFPC would take up would mainly lay outside the orbit of episcopal authority. The World Synod would provide NFPC with a stimulus for promoting an action-oriented convention on justice and peace. The NFPC would attempt to develop an awareness and involvement of grassroots priests in countering the pervasive injustice in our society (Millon, 1971). Denver would be a watershed for the NFPC.

From 'Interests' to 'Values':
A Shift in Policy, 1972–1976

With the Denver convention, the NFPC shifted its emphasis to
wider concerns of pastoral and social ministries. Of the 109 resolutions to be passed in the next three conventions, approximately
sixty-seven would be related to the 'value'-concerns of the NFPC.
Only twenty-four would deal with 'interest' issues, and the remaining would concern the internal affairs of the NFPC. Why the
change? First of all, due process was an accomplished fact in most of
the dioceses. Secondly, in terms of collegiality and shared responsibility, the NFPC felt that this was being accomplished through an
informal mode of operation. The NFPC, being sufficiently institutionalized, was a reality that the NCCB couldn't hide, much less
avoid. Collegiality, in other words, was being accomplished painfully and pragmatically. By sponsoring continuing education and
spiritual workshops, the NFPC had gone far in redefining the
priesthood. The NFPC concluded, after the World Synod meeting in
1971, that the celibacy issue was a dead horse and that to devote any
more time to it would be a waste of energy. Finally, the NFPC felt
that boldness and confrontation relative to 'interest' issues of priests
had been a necessary strategy to dramatize the depressed situation
of priests, but that it was time now to turn one's swords into
plowshares. While some delegate-leaders, especially the more militant association members, didn't agree with this change of emphasis,
it would become the NFPC's general policy for some years to
come.

Thus, the NFPC felt that sufficient victories had been won to
produce a climate for greater freedom, autonomy, and experimentation. Now was the time to pursue in a cooperative manner these
opportunities for leadership and become more accountable to the
ministry. Furthermore, the hierarchy was gradually being replaced
with younger men who were both sensitive to the fellow priests'
needs and supportive of new initiatives. The NFPC itself began to

view the hierarchy on the plus side in terms of working together (see Castelli, 1972b).

DENVER 1972: DOES ANYONE KNOW WHAT REALLY HAPPENED?

The transition from 'interest'-oriented to 'value'-oriented issues, from confrontation to respectability, came into force at the Denver convention. Because the NFPC had been scathed as a result of the 'Moment of Truth' statement, many of the 207 delegates at Denver, representing 127 affiliates, were sensitive to the point of caution in regard to NFPC's image. One indication that the NFPC had tarnished its image was the difficult time it was having collecting dues from its affiliates. Some delegates, for opposite reasons, were estranged from the NFPC's leadership. (See the section on consensus in Chapter 5). The NFPC was trying to find itself in Denver. The delegates were in the doldrums. The NFPC was like a listless ship in the middle of a deadly calm. After the 'Moment of Truth', the NFPC seemed to be experiencing a moment of hesitation.

Thus, the convention moved at a snail's pace because the delegates were on guard to save the NFPC from a 'radical image'. For instance, the same resolution on optional celibacy that passed in Baltimore by a vote of 182 to 23 (89%), was approved in Denver by a vote of only 128 to 70 (65%). The delegates also voted down a resolution allowing membership to the Society of Priests for a Free Ministry, a group dedicated to the cause of married priests. And though the delegates defeated a motion to expel the associations, the more liberal affiliates, from the Federation, the fact that such a motion was even made demonstrates the wariness of many delegates.

There was a certain air of retrenchment present. Father Bonnike felt that, rather than retrenchment, the NFPC was becoming more representative of the rank-and-file priests. The profile data on the Denver delegates in Chapter 4 support this conclusion. It is also a fact that more delegates at this convention were required by their councils to vote a certain way on particular resolutions. In a personal interview with one delegate, he ingloriously referred to the convention as 'the arrival of the Archie Bunkers of the Priesthood'.

While this is a caricature, there is no doubt that the meeting reflected more accurately than ever before the rank-and-file senti-ments. As noted in Chapter 4, the ranks in the American priesthood were much more moderate than the NFPC leaders (see also Castelli, 1972b; Maddock, 1972).

The main focus of the convention was on justice and peace and, although there were no new breakthroughs, the convention did raise the level of awareness of societal oppression and injustice. The theme, that social, economic, and political responsibility were the responsibilities of priests as well as of lay persons, permeated the major addresses. Father Eugene Boyle blasted the 'doctrine of cleavage' and 'theology of rift' which separate the priest from secular matters. He said:

> . . .as Christ, too, it [the Church] must not shrink from this task for fear of getting its hands dirty, or because it may be called bad names . . . . Such a community does not think first of its own survival, of its membership statistics (Castelli, 1972a: 6).

One item of business which caused a moment of whirlwind in the calm was the presidential election. Father Jerome Fraser was sponsored by the more liberal Michigan delegation to run against the incumbent Father Bonnike. Fraser felt that the NFPC was becoming too concerned with the feelings of the bishops. He called for greater autonomy and 'selective disobedience' of bishops. Bon-nike won reelection by 167–33. A consequence of Fraser's can-didacy was to cast Bonnike in a moderate image. And moderation was the spirit of Denver (see Castelli, 1972a: 6).

The policy directives of the NFPC were reflected in Bonnike's 'State of the Federation' address. He described the NFPC's main responsibilities as holding the church establishment accountable and insuring shared responsibility, especially in the area of social justice ministries. He further advised that while 'now is the time for cooperation with the bishops', it is not the time to relinquish newly won autonomies and the freedom to speak for priests' councils. While many of the issues which predominated at Baltimore were actions which the NFPC would champion, Bonnike emphasized the involvement of priests in the plight of the poor, oppressed, and exploited (Bonnike, 1972a). Bonnike said that the two top priorities of the NFPC were to assist in ending the war in Vietnam and in solving the problem of poverty. While the emphasis of the address was on these 'value'-related issues, Bonnike included other areas of concern. There was the need to establish a personnel board, due process machinery, a pension program, and a continuing education program in every diocese. Bonnike urged that if these were not in existence by July 1, 1973, the bishop should resign (see *National Catholic Reporter*, 1972). The NFPC reached a watershed at the Denver convention. It would begin, at first clumsily, to direct most of its energies to the wider issues of the ministry.

Resolutions

There were sixty-two resolutions passed at the Denver meeting. Of these, twenty-four were 'value' issues dealing with social justice and the pastoral ministry, while only fourteen resolutions related to 'interest' issues such as personnel affairs, council structure, bishop-clergy relationships, and continuing education. Twenty-four resolutions dealt with internal affairs of the NFPC, of which ten pertained to the restructuring of the Justice and Peace Committee. (See Table 7.1 near the end of the chapter for a listing of these resolutions.) The resolutions document the shift in policy to 'value'-oriented questions.

The social ministry resolutions dealt with civil rights, economic justice, issues of war and peace, and international justice. The pastoral ministry resolutions related to such matters as ministry to homosexuals, alternative ministries, marriage legislation, the abortion issue, and public religious education. The 'interest' resolutions dealt with the same problems treated in previous conventions, such as optional celibacy, laicization, priests' life style, selection and tenure of bishops, and continuing educational programs. (See Appendix D for a complete itemization of these and the Detroit and San Fransisco resolutions.) Of significance at this convention was the fact that each resolution which was introduced called for some specific action to be implemented in the home diocese (*Priests-USA*, 1972d).

NFPC: 1972–1973

While one would correctly predict an emphasis on pastoral and social ministerial concerns, the NFPC nevertheless continued to involve itself with 'interest' issues. Work in the area of justice and peace was largely conceived in terms of insuring that local councils could work effectively in this area.

The NFPC's Office of Justice and Peace was strengthened by the employment of a full-time director, Father Eugene Boyle. In August, Boyle released an action program for local councils. This included organizational efforts assisting local councils to set up justice and peace committees. While criticizing the U.S. political and economic system because it 'cannot guarantee us a generation of peace', Father Boyle stated that the NFPC's function must be to stimulate a new populism (*Priests-USA*, 1972i). Specifically, the NFPC intensified its involvement with the cause of the United Farm Workers. The Justice and Peace Office vigorously fought California's Proposition 22, which was intended to prevent boycotting (*Priests-USA*, 1972m: 1).

Another significant area of involvement was corporate responsibility and church investments. In July of 1972, NFPC announced a research project which was to develop the moral principles by which church investment performance could be evaluated. It was also intended to produce models for investment review and to educate local councils regarding this issue. By March, 1973, NFPC had joined with nine other Catholic organizations to form the National Catholic Coalition for Responsible Investment. It sponsored traveling workshops designed for consciousness-raising on the topic of theology of investment and church responsibility (*Priests-USA*, 1973a: 1).

The NFPC also began efforts toward pastoral accountability and ministerial effectiveness. Much of this effort went into establishing and strengthening contacts with other Catholic organizations such as the National Association of Women Religious, the Leadership Conference of Women Religious, the Conference of Major Superiors of Men, the National Assembly of Religious Brothers, and the Federation of Catholic Seminarians (Mayo, 1973a: 2–3). This area of accountability would become the theme of the NFPC's convention in Detroit.

The NFPC continued to show interest in issues which had been predominant at previous conventions. In May, 1972, Bonnike met with the School of Canon Law at the Catholic University of America. Topics discussed were familiar ones: shared decision making, selection of bishops, protection of priests' rights, clergy remuneration, celibacy, the permanent diaconate, and pastoral accountability (*Priests-USA*, 1972g: 1). Other NFPC developments included the completion of a national survey of priests' incomes, endorsement of the Parish Evaluation Program (PEP), the establishment of a national pension plan for church personnel entitled 'Personnel Group Benefit Trust', a clergy distribution research project, and prayer symposia.

The Federation was also responsible for initiating both the National Association of Church Personnel Administrators and the National Organization for Continuing Education of Roman Catholic Clergy. The latter organization, incidentally, was in response to the NCCB document entitled 'the Program of Continuing Education of Priests' (Mayo, 1973a: 2).

Except in one instance which I will discuss later, the tone of the NFPC leadership regarding 'interest' issues and programs was moderate and conciliatory. For instance, in clarifying the NFPC's stand regarding the selection of bishops, Bonnike explained that the NFPC favors a more representative voice for priests, religious, and laity in the nomination process for bishops, but does not support a totally democratic selection process (Bonnike, 1972b: 2).

Bonnike continued to address the issue of optional celibacy by stating that the Church cannot demand that a person surrender an inalienable right (freedom to marry) for a lifetime. He further stated that the Church has an "obligation in justice" to those priests who have married and wish to continue service to the church (Bonnike, 1972c).

The issue of the celibacy norm and its dispensation soon occupied the front burner again. On June 26, the Sacred Congregation for the Doctrine of the Faith issued a rescript tightening the procedures for priests' resignations. In effect, the decree stated that the desire to marry was not sufficient grounds for dispensations. In strong language, Bonnike, acting on his own initiative, denounced the rescript as 'punitive' and condemned its authors for their hypocrisy and ulterior motives (Bonnike, 1972d). Father Eugene Kennedy concurred with Bonnike, stating that the rescript denies freedom and that it is the authors of the document who are estranged from Christianity (*Priests-USA*, 1972l: 1). The November issue of *Priests-USA* (1972n) reported that priests responded 6 to 1 in favor of Bonnike's charges, citing the main reasons for opposing the rescript as violation of human dignity and disrespect for the woman's role in the church. In regard to women's rights, it is important to note that the delegates at the Denver convention voted to support the ordination of women (*Priests-USA*, 1972e).

The NFPC continued to respond to charges that its structure did not allow it to properly represent priests. Bonnike, in response to Father Munzing's 'blueprint' of criticisms, pointed out that the NFPC did not claim to represent all American priests; rather it spoke for priests' councils who do represent the rank and file. Monsignor Joseph Baker and Father Joel Munzing continued to criticize the NFPC as unrepresentative and charged the NFPC with granting membership to unofficial organizations (associations), with being self-serving, and with having an influence which is wholly negative. In an editorial (*Priests-USA*, 1972j), the NFPC stated that, though it wasn't perfect, it was, for better or for worse, the only representative organization existing for priests in the United States.

The NFPC experienced a change in leadership, when, in January, 1973, Father Bonnike announced his resignation. No reasons were given for this decision (Bonnike, 1973), but one could infer that Bonnike was under great pressure. There was substantial negative reaction to his response to the rescript on resignations of priests, even from his own diocesan council. There were also continual charges that the NFPC was unrepresentative. Finally, there was the question and quandary concerning the purpose and functions of the NFPC once the NCCB had established its national Office of Priestly Life and Ministry. Bonnike had previously recommended to the Executive Board nine structural possibilities for the continuance of the NFPC. One of the more significant options was that the NFPC, while retaining certain autonomies such as selection of its leadership, would become part of the NCCB's organization, USCC. The Executive Board was at variance with Bonnike on this issue.

NFPC AND THE BISHOPS

In April, 1972, Bonnike reported a hopeful note in regard to NFPC-NCCB relations. He stated that the NFPC was in constant contact with the NCCB and its committees. In July, an editorial (*Priests-USA*, 1972h) spoke to those who would have the NFPC take a more confrontative stance with the NCCB. It emphasized that the NFPC's goal was collaboration, rather than confrontation, with the NCCB, but that the NFPC would still confront the NCCB when the need arose. The April NCCB meeting, however, was a great disappointment to the NFPC.

> It is our consideration that meaningful episcopal dialogue was wanting . . . because all but a handful of the proponents of change elected to be silent and accept the more aggressive tactics of the champions of the status quo (*Priests-USA*, 1972f).

Observers at the NCCB meeting were blocked from proceedings which they had been told they could attend. A further complaint was the continued postponement of the publication of the NCCB's studies on the priesthood.

Observers to the November NCCB meeting, however, were glad to see an emphasis on 'value' issues, such as Bishop Hurley's call for leadership from the bishops on the issue of human values and technology, attention to the plight of the Spanish-speaking people, and the establishment of a Committee on Priestly Life and Ministry. But there were disappointments. Cardinal Krol had given little direction in regard to amnesty and the NCCB's statement on the Indochina war was described as an 'innocuous word game'. The situation of farm workers was largely overlooked. It was also reported that, out of twenty secretariats of the Committee on Research, Plans, and Programs, fifteen had neither new programs nor plans to report (*Priests-USA*, 1972: 1). In summary, the NFPC was softening its approach to the NCCB. It felt that progress was being made in terms of communications, if not collaboration. The NCCB began to accept the existence of the NFPC in a pragmatic way, but it was still suspicious and fearful of the NFPC since it had no control over its policy and deliberations.

NFPC and Local Council Leadership

In a progress report on NFPC provinces and member councils, the formidable problem for the provinces was called 'a conspiracy to do nothing'. The most common problems seemed to be organizational in nature: leadership, organizational skills, effective regional meetings, diocesan planning, and a parochial outlook (*Priests-USA*, 1972k).

As mentioned in Chapter 5, the NFPC initially had been more successful in consolidating the minds and hearts of local council representatives than in effecting unity in collaboration and communication. Its influence on the local councils was modest; its influence was even less on the local bishop. Yet it was highly effective in becoming a representative voice and was successful in the due process issue. Then came Denver. The 1972 data showed that, while the NFPC still had a high degree of consensus and cohesion, it wasn't effective in maintaining this level, especially in regard to agreement on leadership approaches and policy directions. At the same time, these delegates reported some improvement in collaboration and communication between the NFPC and its affiliates. These representatives also stated that the influence of the NFPC on the local council and the bishop had grown. In terms of goal attainment, the greatest progress in 1972 was related to 'value'-oriented goals. The NFPC continued both its policy of emphasizing 'value' questions and its cooperative approach throughout 1973.

Detroit 1973: Tensions in Accountability

The turbulent years of the NFPC seemed to be over. There was a new mood within the NFPC calling for active collaboration with all segments of the church, especially with the bishops. The approach of the new NFPC president, Father Reid Mayo, and the softening of militant tactics during the previous year, gave the impression that the Federation was striking a balance. Mayo stated:

If groups threatened to secede, scornful of the toned-down voice that a maturing NFPC had developed over the past six years, they would have to do so. The determination of the NFPC to present a responsive image to the bishops was not going to falter (Mahoney, 1973: 149).

The theme 'Tensions in Accountability' certainly wasn't the language of confrontation and militancy. There were and would be tensions, for the NFPC still addressed itself to relevant issues dealing with priests' interests and ministerial experimentations while, at the same time, centering its activity on 'orthodox' issues that would command the hierarchy's cooperation. During a wintry week in Detroit, the assembly of 225 delegates and alternates, representing 131 councils, attempted to attain this balance. The March blizzard that met the delegates had a stormy counterpart in their three days of deliberations. Tensions there were, not between the NFPC and the NCCB, but among the delegates themselves. Certain issues, such as celibacy and women in the ministry, revealed that the NFPC leadership was, in the words of John Mahoney (1973), '. . . an unstable and sometimes volatile coalition of opposing groups'. The issue of celibacy was a case in point. The Detroit resolution did not request a change in the celibacy law, but called for a survey of the laity's reaction to a married priesthood. One will recall the strongly worded resolution which passed in Baltimore by a vote of 182 to 23 (89%), and a similar resolution approved in Denver, although only by a vote of 128 to 70 (65%). Now, a harmless resolution on celibacy was passed by a vote of only 106 to 67 (61%). Moderation was the spirit of the convention, at least in regard to 'interest' issues of the priesthood. (See *America*, 1973.)

Father Mayo embodied this new spirit of moderation. He evidenced a political maturity which maintained the autonomy of the NFPC while embarking on a road of active cooperation with the U.S. hierarchy. Mayo's efforts were strengthened by the welcoming comments of Cardinal Dearden who said, in calling for collaboration, 'We [the bishops] can't do it alone and neither can you [NFPC]' (Castelli, 1973b: 1).

Accountability of the priesthood was stressed in Mayo's 'State of the Federation' address. He stated:

Mature interdependence, exercised in a responsible collegial manner, is urgently necessary if we are to address ourselves to the needs of God's people. . . . Perhaps the greatest injustice that we perpetrate on one another is not trusting each other enough to allow for the process of becoming . . . . How often we are prone to deciding, based only on assumptions, just who a person is, and then take away his freedom by not allowing him to become and grow (Mayo, 1973: 3).

This notion of accountability was echoed by Bishop Remi De Roo of Victoria, British Columbia, who said:

Accountability implies sufficient freedom so that my actions or omissions are under control of my reason and will. It also supposes an obligation . . . to exercise that freedom (Castelli, 1973b: 1).

Much of the convention was devoted to the personal accountability and evaluation of priests in order to facilitate both their professional competence and their ministerial effectiveness. In a sense, this policy emphasis on professional accountability in the ministry is a revolutionary theme. Priests have never had to answer, in a systematic way, about their ministerial effectiveness. Application of this policy will no doubt bring tensions to the priesthood. One speaker touched on this point specifically. Father Gill, a psychiatrist at Harvard University, said:

. . . it must be obvious . . . that we can expect the most intense opposition to a system of accountability will be put forward by those priests who have been in the past most ineffective. . . . Those who have not reached a stage of maturity and dedication which would prompt them to make whatever sacrifices are entailed in order to serve their people as well as they possibly can (Gill, 1973: 13–15).

The delegates were also told that they must face up to their accountability to women in the ministry. Bishop De Roo told the priests that:

. . . the mystery of salvation . . . cannot be fully lived while women are restrained in their service to the ministry. . . . We priests and bishops will be failing in our accountability unless and until we recognize the full partnership of woman as a sister to man (Castelli, 1973a).

Sister Francis Borgia Rothluebber, president of the School Sisters of St. Francis, called for a releasing of the 'feminine' qualities in the church and the 'free-flowing, wholesome relationships between men and women' in the Church. While the delegates supported a proposal furthering the role of women in the ministry, they were not willing at this time to accept equal status of women in the ministry, as evidenced by the defeated motion calling for the ordination of women (Castelli, 1973a).

Elaborating on accountability, Father Mayo reminded the delegates that the NFPC was accountable to its founding goals (see Appendix I) and stressed the accountability of the affiliates and of the priests belonging to the local councils to work toward these goals (Mayo, 1973a: 1).

In outlining the future efforts of the NFPC, Mayo emphasized justice and peace issues, such as renewed efforts on behalf of the farm workers, investment accountability and corporate responsibility, initiation of a peace education program, support of legislation to improve poverty programs, and the study of new types of ministries. Other areas of concern were the strengthening of provincial structures, cooperation with local pastoral councils and the Office of Priestly Life and Ministry, distribution of clergy, and a clergy retirement policy (Mayo, 1973a: 3–4).

The NFPC delegates were also brought up to date on the NCCB's Office of Priestly Life and Ministry. Monsignor MacDonald, the pro-tem executive director of the committee, criticized those who felt that the office would replace the NFPC. He said that the Federation has been an important rallying point for priests and should continue as one. He also said that it was needed for what it could do in cooperation with the bishops' conference and as an advocate of social and ecclesial programs in the U.S. (Castelli, 1973b: 15).

The NFPC had reached a plane of political realism in Detroit. The NFPC would continue to direct its policy to wider 'value' concerns of the ministry. To be effective in the pastoral and social ministry, it would stress both personal and organizational accountability to foster the renewal of the Church and society.

Resolutions

There were twenty-three resolutions passed at the Detroit meeting. Sixteen dealt with the 'value' concerns of justice and peace and ministerial activity; only five resolutions were related to 'interest' issues of the priesthood. Two were about the internal affairs of the NFPC.

The NFPC voted to establish a peace education program using the World Without War Council as a consultant. The program would act as a catalyst, aiding other Catholic structures in the justice and peace field by providing research, planning, the program functions to local councils. Guidelines for ethical investments and corporate responsibility, which had been developed during the past year, were implemented in a resolution concerned with the Federation's share of stock in General Electric: at the next shareholders' meeting, the NFPC would vote in favor of establishing a committee on economic conversion. Another resolution called upon the affiliates to join in organizational efforts to back the rights of the poor who were the targets of administration cutbacks. Other 'value' issues dealt with prison reform, amnesty, support for social justice movements, solidarity with oppressed people in Latin America, justice at Wounded Knee, opposition to abortion, and alternative ministries.

The 'interest' resolutions dealt with optional celibacy and the laicization process, priest distribution, and bishop-clergy relations. It is clear that the shift of the NFPC's policy which began in Denver continued to expand in the area of commonweal concerns.

A YEAR WITH THE UNITED FARM WORKERS OF AMERICA

Father Mayo, to a large extent, set the tone for NFPC policy directions in an article which set forth the major goals of the NFPC as the attainment of peace and harmony in relationships with others. In this context, he emphasized the need for respect, trust, and honesty (Mayo, 1973b). He elaborated on this theme in an address to the priests' councils and bishops of Region XII in Spokane, in October, 1973. His emphasis here was on leadership as an open, candid observation, communication, and guidance. Leadership was defined as collegiality and guidance, mutual recognition and respect (Mayo, 1973c). But all was not peaceful. The drama and controversy, however, was not within the arena of episcopal authority, but in the vineyards of California.

NFPC's involvement with the UFWA dominated 1973. On June 29, more than twenty priest, including Father Mayo, lined up with UFWA workers during a strike at Coachella, California. This NFPC action was initiated by Father Boyle, NFPC Justice and Peace director. On July 31, more than forty priests were arrested, along with many farm workers, for violating an injunction that prohibited pickets from assembling within a hundred feet of one another. All the priests agreed to remain in jail until the farm workers were released (*Priests-USA*, 1973g).

In another NFPC activity of major importance, the National Catholic Coalition for Responsible Investment initiated its first symposium in April at Milwaukee. The workshop stressed the ethical principles involved in church investments. The Church's primary responsibility is not profits, but to insure that corporations are serving the common good. Also in April, Father Mayo spoke at the General Electric stockholders meeting supporting a resolution that asked General Electric to establish a committee on economic conversion (*Priests-USA*, 1973c).

Mandated at the Detroit convention, the NFPC established a program of peace education designed to establish a training program, coordinate NFPC justice and peace projects, and work with other Catholic organizations in this endeavor. In July, it also announced the establishment of a task force on prison reform. Its purpose was to develop a statement of theological and sociological principles regarding prison reform and to design models of action for local councils (*Priests-USA*, 1973e).

The NFPC was concerned both with informing councils about local actions in regard to pertinent issues of the priesthood and ministry and the utilization of priests who have resigned from the ministry. In order to implement this concern, the NFPC Personnel Committee established both a clearinghouse of information and a *Search and Share Directory*. The former was designed with the intention of assisting the Church in utilizing the services of resigned priests. The latter was to make available successful diocesan programs, policies, and instruments to member councils (*Priests-USA*, 1973f).

To assist in the professional growth of priests, the NFPC began to establish ties with the Catholic University of America during the fall of 1973. The important proposals centered around a sabbatical continuing education program and a training program, sponsored by the Catholic University of America, for chairmen of local councils' Research and Development Committees (*Priests-USA*, 1973i: 1).

A major concern of the NFPC was the problem of representation of religious order priests. Nearly half of the priests in the country belonged to religious orders; yet only a handful of religious order councils were affiliated with the NFPC. At Baltimore, the delegates had addressed themselves to this imbalance by encouraging the admittance of religious orders. Following the Detroit meeting, an eleven-man caucus of religious order priests sent a letter to all the U.S. religious superiors asking them to initiate discussions regarding affiliation with the NFPC. Research on religious order representation in diocesan councils revealed that the religious were underrepresented by 50% of their number and that the barriers to representation were both the lack of motivation by religious and structural deficiencies on the part of the councils (Stewart, 1973a).

BISHOPS BEGIN TO LISTEN

The period between the Detroit and San Francisco conventions was characterized by more cooperation and less conflict between the NFPC and the NCCB than at any previous time. MacDonald, executive director of the NCCB ad hoc Committee on Priestly Life and Ministry, stated: '. . . officially the NFPC is still considered a non-entity by the NCCB. Unofficially, there has been a tremendous amount of liaison and dialogue'. He went on to say that the NFPC is needed as a cooperative element with the NCCB (*Priests-USA*, 1973b). Reports of regional meetings of the bishops indicated that, by and large, the hierarchy no longer saw collegiality as a threat. Instead of closed doors, most regional meetings revealed that the bishops were listening to both priests and laity (*Priests-USA*, 1973d).

While observers at the November NCCB meeting felt that it lacked sufficient free and open dialogue, they did feel that the work of the regional meetings was having an effect on the bishops. For instance, the NCCB moved into the area of prison reform, issued a statement concerning the Middle East War, and unanimously endorsed a motion to support the UFWA strike and boycott (*Priests-USA*, 1973h). Another indication that the NCCB was beginning to respond to the NFPC and priests in general was an announcement in January, 1974, in which the NCCB called for broad consultation in the submission of names of candidates for executive secretary of the permanent Committee on Priestly Life and Ministry. Moreover, priests would be selected as consultants to the Committee (*Priests-USA*, 1974a).

SAN FRANCISCO 1974: A REASON FOR HOPE

The NFPC was founded in a turbulent era for both the Church and society. There was a polarization between priests and bishops. Priests were demanding their rights as persons and searching for leadership to bring about a renewal of spirit and structure. The American society was also shattered by urban riots and protests against a war described as immoral. It seemed as though dissent was about to destroy the unity required for the survival of church and society. Immorality and injustice had been institutionalized in law and custom. Yet change had to come about lest human dignity and freedom be destroyed. These were big problems.

Who would be bold enough to take on the establishment? Who would be wise enough to discern that much of the oppression in the church and society was a result of paternalistic neglect? The rhetoric of 'power to the people' got to the core issue of the 1960s more than many people were willing to admit. The NFPC became one response to this crisis of self-determination. At the New Orleans convention, which started the NFPC off on an agenda for action, Father O'Malley said that the NFPC was a sign of hope to the priest who was experiencing doubts and frustrations about the Church, the priesthood, and himself.

The NFPC returned to this theme in San Francisco, 1974. 'Priests-USA: A reason for hope . . . Si, se puede!' was largely a reflection of the current status of the NFPC. In 1974 the NFPC, whose very existence, as well as its activities, had long been surrounded by controversy and opposition, could point to both a long list of accomplishments and increasing recognition by priests and hierarchy alike.

In serving the needs of the priesthood, the ministry, and the wider society, the influence of the NFPC on local councils and the NCCB had grown in a positive way. Although this influence, sometimes direct but more often subtle, is hard to measure, it is doubtful that recent local council initiatives or developments in the NCCB regarding social justice and the ministry would have taken place without the NFPC.

The NFPC had emphasized during its first four years of existence the concerns and interests of priests relative to their status and rights in the power structure of the Church. Judging that these issues were on their way toward solution, it changed its direction in 1972 toward wider issues of the common good. This emphasis was again evident in San Francisco when over 200 delegates, representing 130 councils, came to deliberate the major social issues of the day. The de-emphasis on the internal welfare issues of priests may in the future cause problems for the NFPC. While personnel and due process issues have been achieved, shared leadership and responsibility on national and diocesan levels are still problems. Many of the experienced delegates seemed to be of the opinion that priests of the nation were seriously in need of a vision of hope and leadership. They were tired of the bishops making a major issue of a non-issue like communion-in-the-hand while neglecting the economic and political corruption found in American establishments (*Priests-USA*, 1974b). In the estimation of many priests, the way for enlightened and courageous leadership to develop was through team leadership and collegiality. The full realization of this goal is still in the future.

Perhaps the NFPC will be a sign of hope also for this segment of the priesthood. The NFPC realizes that there is still a leadership vacuum in the U.S. Church. In his 'State of the Federation' address, Father Mayo referred to this situation by saying:

The Church today is looking for new forms of leadership. . . . The NFPC is becoming . . . the vehicle whereby the Church, through its priests particularly, can come up with new directions, fresh ideas, and new insights (Joyce, 1974).

The most newsworthy issue of the convention was the rights of homosexuals. The approved resolutions called for the development of a theology of homosexuality; opposed all civil laws that make consentual homosexual acts between adults a crime; and objected to discrimination against homosexuals in employment, governmental service, housing, and child-rearing which involves either natural or adoptive parents. But the delegates rejected a call on the Catholic Church to end discrimination against homosexuals in its own employment practices.

The Executive Board voted not to release a report, prepared by the Salvatorian Fathers' task force, on the ministry to homosexuals. Father Mayo said that, based on reactions to the report by Father Charles Curran, professor of moral theology at Catholic University, and by Father Eugene Kennedy, professor of psychology at Loyola University of Chicago, the Board had decided that the theological aspects of the report were undeveloped (*National Catholic Reporter*, 1974: 24).

In light of the evidence presented in this book, one would not expect to find the NFPC on the brink of another controversy involving the authority of the hierarchy. The potential controversy, this time around, involved a 'value' issue as opposed to the past controversies of the NFPC. One explanation of why such a document (stating that homosexuality is theologically good) came before the House of Delegates is that the leadership of this report was from a religious order council which has specialized in alternative forms of the ministry. And it is a fact of Church life that religious orders are more free and flexible in their ministry than diocesan priests; thus the potential for controversy.

Yet 'newsworthiness' does not denote the dominant concerns of the delegates and the significance of the 1974 convention. The salient features of the convention were both the spirit of sensitive concern and the competency demonstrated in addressing social justice and ministerial concerns. The warmth that greeted Cesar Chavez and the enthusiastic reaction to Father Dwyer's address on spiritual formation and the ministry reflected these priorities (see Egan, 1974).

Except for intense debates over the issues of homosexuality and the resolutions calling for the impeachment of President Nixon and increased priests' participation in political affairs, the convention moved along in a methodical, business-like way. In his 'State of the Federation' address, President Mayo echoed the spirit of the deliberations by saying, 'There is hope in the patient steady efforts to resolve controversies and to achieve reconciliation' (Mayo, 1974a: 38).

Most likely Mayo and the NFPC leadership had come to the realization that the NFPC was crossing a new threshold which could be called 'institutionalized recalcitrance'. As with many other social movements, such as the civil rights effort, the NFPC initially began to dramatize the injustices within the Church. Victories came relatively quickly, if not easily. Some issues of priests were solved only in part or not at all, such as co-responsibility and celibacy. The NFPC, to maintain its momentum, moved on to wider and more complex issues of social justice and the common good. Most of these issues were 'biggies' in the society's system of responsibility and ethics.

Within this framework, injustice, oppression, racism, and denial of human rights were everyone's fault and nobody's responsibility. To get out of this bureaucratic paralysis demanded replacement models and norms. The effort to tear down and replace irrelevant and immoral norms of the status quo would be met by the recalcitrance of institutional behavior. A great deal of defense would be personal and protective, for no one wants to freely relinquish power and prestige. But the most potent enemy of church renewal and societal reform is the blind stubbornness of large-scale institutionalization which can only produce dull managers of stability rather than wise leaders of innovation.

The NFPC seems to have come to the decision that organizational recalcitrance to shared leadership and world justice could only be confronted by 'patient steady efforts'.

Efforts for the year would be mounted on many fronts. Although Father Boyle resigned as the full-time director of the NFPC Office of Justice and Peace, the NFPC continued to work diligently in the defense of the powerless, Blacks, Indians, and farm workers; to educate and train leaders for peace. Mayo encouraged member councils to find ways to utilize the talents of priests who had resigned; to establish constructive, collaborative ventures with other church organizations; to strengthen the provincial structures; to work with sisters' and pastoral councils in effecting collegiality; and to develop leadership within their own ranks (Mayo, 1974b). Mayo's emphasis throughout the 'State of the Federation' speech was on the NFPC as a facilitator of collaboration, both in the church and in society.

A new twist has developed in the NFPC's policy. It involves a new definition, or rather a redefinition, of the function of the NFPC. Over the years the NFPC's policies have shifted in emphasis from 'interest' to 'value' questions, but almost always it was acting alone in spearheading innovation. It is now beginning to see itself as a communicative and collaborative exchange system, building up a network of relations with other organizations. Regardless of the issue, be it a 'value'-related or 'interest'-related question, the NFPC is viewing itself both as a promoter of inter-organizational effort and as a generator of 'new directions, fresh ideas, and new insights'. The leadership may have had this in mind during the past two years when it decided on a policy of keeping the NFPC organizationally 'trim and tidy'. Instead of elaborating an administrative bureaucracy, the NFPC launched, as independent organizations, the work of personnel boards' administrators, continuing education directors, and the work of the National Catholic Coalition for Responsible Investment. This allowed the Federation time for research and reflection.

Over the years, the NFPC's research arm, under the direction of Fathers Larry Wiskirchen and Don Bargen, has greatly influenced NFPC directions and programs. These projects included the studies of priestly celibacy, clergy distribution, an evaluation of NFPC's effectiveness, studies of the remuneration of clergy, the ethics of church investment, religious order representation, evaluation of provincial structures, and vocational recruitment. Research has been carried on by other committees also, such as the 'Search and Share' directory, guidelines for personnel boards, assessments of diocesan efforts in the area of justice and peace, and continuing education.

The NFPC has seen well-informed judgments as requisite for effectiveness in developing creative ministries. It will intensify this effort during 1974 by seeking foundation support for its research and programs (Mayo, 1974a: 34). Most likely the NFPC will continue to expand the functions of creating and communicating ideas for more effective programs.

Resolutions

Of the twenty-four resolutions passed in San Francisco, seventeen were related to 'value' questions of social justice and pastoral ministries; only five dealt with 'interest' issues of the priesthood. Two dealt with the internal affairs of the Federation. (See Table 7.1 for the summary listing of resolutions. See Appendix D for a comparative itemization of all resolutions for the past six years.)

The major social justice resolutions dealt with amnesty, the arms race, racism, prison reform, corporate responsibility, political participation by the clergy, and impeachment of the president. Resolutions on ministerial concerns were related to homosexual issues, divorce, teaching of religious values in public schools, use of the 'Search and Share' directory, rural ministry, annointing of alcoholics, and ministerial cooperation with other organizations.

The 'interest' resolutions dealt with the selection of bishops, continuing education, laicization, and an evaluative study of the NFPC. Thus one sees the ever-expanding concern of the NFPC for the broader issues of the common good.

The graph in Table 7.2 provides the reader with a clear picture of the policy trends of the NFPC. 'Interest' issues captured the NFPC's attention in the beginning, dominated its activity up to 1972, and then sharply dropped as issues of major concern. On the other hand, the 'value' issues received less attention in the beginning, but gradually became more important in the ensuing years.

NFPC: 1974–1975

The major thrust continued to be issues of justice and peace. The week of April 28 to May 4 was designated as National Farm Worker Week and Mayo called for increased support of the boycott. The National Catholic Coalition for Responsible Investment conducted symposia in six ecclesiastical regions. The NFPC also addressed the

Table 7.1   *Resolutions passed at NFPC annual conventions*

	1969–71* (N = 111)	1972 (N = 62)	1973 (N = 23)	1974 (N = 24)	1972–74 (N = 109)
JUSTICE AND PEACE	27	13	13	10	36
1. Civil rights	2	2	2	3	7
2. Economic justice	10	5	6	2	13
3. War and peace	10	4	3	2	9
4. International justice	2	2	1	1	4
5. Political justice	0	0	1	2	3
6. Community organization and needs	3	0	0	0	0
MINISTRY AND PRIESTLY LIFE	29	14	6	8	28
1. Normative interests of priests	22	3	3	1	7
2. Ministerial concerns	3	5	1	6	12
3. Alternative ministries	4	6	2	1	9
PERSONNEL	30	7	2	2	11
1. Accountability and evaluation	11	3	0	0	3
2. Research and development on priest distribution	1	1	1	1	3
3. Bishop-clergy relations	18	3	1	1	5
COMMUNICATIONS	1	1	0	0	1
RESEARCH AND DEVELOPMENT	0	1	0	0	2
FINANCE	7	3	1	1	5
PRIESTS' COUNCILS AND LAITY	6	2	0	1	3
1. Pastoral Councils	4	1	0	0	1
2. Evaluation	2	1	0	1	2
CONTINUING EDUCATION	3	2	0	1	3
CONSTITUTION AND INTERNAL AFFAIRS	8	19	1	1	21

* For the detailed figures for the years 1969, 1970 and 1971, see Table 6.1.

annual stockholder meeting of General Electric. Father Steve Adrian, the NFPC's representative, asked G E to evaluate each proposed project in terms of environmental and energy conservation. Also, Father Patrick Carney, the NFPC's represenative on the board of IMPACT (an interfaith legislative network) asked priests' councils to petition Congress to cut military expenditures. Other

Table 7.2 *Trends of 'interest' and 'values' resolutions*

Number of resolutions	New Orleans 1969	San Diego 1970	Baltimore 1971	Denver 1972	Detroit 1973	San Francisco 1974

```
30
25
20
15
10
 5
 0
```

— = 'Interests' resolutions.
- - - = 'Values' resolutions.

social justice activities taken up by the NFPC during 1974 included (1) an invitation to all councils to participate in a campaign against the U.S. government B-1 supersonic bomber, (2) the launching of the 'World Without War' program, (3) taking the position in favor of unconditional amnesty for war resisters and developing an educational program addressed to this issue, and (4) authorizing the hiring of a full-time Justice and Peace director. The Justice and Peace Committee also continued its working relations with the Catholic Committee on Urban Ministry, National Farm Workers Ministry, and the Inter-religious Foundation for Community Organization.

In the pastoral ministry area, the NFPC developed resource materials for use by priests' councils in the selection of bishops. The guidebook contains suggested procedures for prior consultation regarding candidates for the episcopacy. In other actions, (1) the NFPC produced a research report on religious values in public schools; (2) prepared a study on the diocesan collegial structure: the relationship among the pastoral council, priests' council, and the bishop; (3) called for the restoration of the diaconate for women; (4) expanded the *Search and Share Directory;* (5) cosponsored with the National Center for Church Vocations an in depth study of changing values in vocation recruitment; and (6) launched the first leadership training workshop for presidents of local councils.

The NFPC, the Glenmary Fathers, and the National Catholic Rural Life Conference initiated a national collaborative program to address the needs of rural America. The program calls for affiliated local councils to sponsor workshops on the social, political, economic, and religious aspects of rural issues, their relation to the rural experience and the Church's role in it (*Priests-USA*, 1974e).

RELATIONS WITH THE BISHOPS

Tensions in reciprocity were still in evidence between the NFPC and the bishops. Archbishop Jean Jadot, U.S. Apostolic Delegate, addressed a special message to NFPC President Mayo expressing his concern over bishop-priest polarization. He cited the need for solidarity and collegiality in the context of respect and patience (*Priests-USA*, 1974c). About the same time, Bishop Thomas Grady, chairman of the NCCB Committee on Priestly Life and Ministry, stated that his committee has no intention of co-opting the NFPC, but recognizes the NFPC as a significant organization in the work of co-responsibility. In June, the Committee on Priestly Life and Ministry held its first meeting. Father Mayo was one of the twelve priest-consultants in attendance. Topics discussed were continuing education of priests with an emphasis on spirituality, values of priests as compared to secular values, new forms of ministry, and the strengthening of senates (*Priests-USA*, 1974d).

The election of Archbishop Joseph Bernadin to the NCCB presidency in the fall of 1974 symbolized the emergence of a new leadership among the bishops. Bernadin called for a new cooperation among bishops, priests, religious, and laity to participate in the transformation of the world on behalf of justice. A symbol of this fresh emphasis on collegiality was the call to the Catholic community to join the bishops in observing two days of fast every week. Also, the well-received report of the Committee on Priestly Life and Ministry points to serious cooperation with priests and the NFPC (*Priests-USA*, 1974f).

THE ST. PETERSBURG CONVENTION: 1975

The theme of the 1975 convention was 'Reconciliation: Risks and Possibilities'. Five dominant areas in need of reconciliation were determined by the NFPC leadership as judged by feedback of eighty percent of the member councils. The areas selected by the affiliates were: (1) distribution of world resources, (2) alienated youth, (3) liberal-conservative Catholics, (4) divorced and remarried Catholics, and (5) resigned priests.

A new convention format, which will be used in future meetings, allowed a more extensive participation in the decision-making process. Each delegate to the convention was equipped with re-source materials in one of the five focal areas of concern. During the first two days of the convention, he along with a selected number of other delegates devoted their time exclusively to developing a working plan of action. A drafting committee designed a total statement incorporating the five plans of action. On Wednesday the statement was reviewed and amended at provincial meetings of the delegates, then sent on for parliamentary debate on Wednesday afternoon and evening. Thus, the convention took on the air of a workshop devoid of major speeches. The only experts present were resource persons for each of the five focal concerns. The delegates passed four of the five units in the working paper, while assigning the liberal-conservative area to a task force for further study.

Although the working paper on reconciliation is not a policy statement, it does give general directions to the member councils' agendas for 1975–1976. Major items of this plan of action include: (1) call for members of local councils to pledge 10% of their individual gross incomes for one year to help feed the world's hungry; (2) mandate a full-time NFPC justice and peace director and call on local councils to plan a wide range of educational programs in the area of world hunger; (3) request that U.S. Bishops consider lifting the excommunication sanction of divorced-remarried Catholics and urge that, out of respect for the primacy of conscience, exclusion from the Eucharist no longer apply to parties in a second marriage; and (4) urge consultation between the NFPC and the NCCB to find ways to reconcile and reinstate married priests in appropriate ministries (*Priests-USA*, 1975a).

Besides the issues of reconciliation found in the working paper, there were two resolutions passed at the Florida convention. One urged Congressmen to support a national health insurance bill which would incorporate a respect for the 'primary right' of life for unborn as well as born infants. The other resolution gave support to the United Farm Workers' boycott of Gallo Wines. The full weight of the NFPC was put behind the 'value' issues of the commonweal both in the wider society and the Church. There was the call of reconciliation; a call to recognize, respect, and reciprocate with such diverse groups as alienated youth, divorced Catholics, reactionaries of the right and the left, resigned priests, and the poor of the world. Implementing this agenda of action will certainly cause tensions and conflicts. This was foreseen by Father Mayo and noted in his state of the Federation address (Mayo, 1975):

> Will this reconciliation involve risks? Indeed, it will. Some clergy and laity will not understand, some will threaten, some will withdraw. Giving the 'liberal' an equal standing in a conservative congregation, or acknowledging the leadership of a 'conservative' in a liberal community will be disturbing to some. Going out to the alienated youth may cause some to take scandal. Publicly showing respect and special ministry to the resigned priest will cause many to fear that other priests will be encouraged to leave the active ministry.
>
> Reconciliation with the divorced and remarried will require less concern about scandal and more flexibility in marriage cases and certain changes which will appear to some as arbitrary. And the poor—can we not give them the privileged place they have in the Gospel? It will hurt to sacrifice—and they will not always be grateful.
>
> Many will object that this approach will disregard justice, upset the 'faithful', undermine good order and seemingly encourage disregard for the law. Some will not understand that the dogma and revealed truths of the faith are one thing—for example, with regard to the indissolubility of marriage—while the pastoral practices are oftentimes another. Undoubtedly these are dangers, but dangers that are small in comparison to the danger of being a people of hardened hearts.

The controversies which the NFPC will embark on during the next several years will continue to lie in the pathway of 'value' concerns of justice and equality as against the 'interest' issues of priests' rights.

By the Denver convention, the NFPC had ceased to be a militant social movement regarding priests' issues. The rights and benefits of priests were no longer its primary concern. In terms of social justice issues, it became one more organization joining the fight to end oppression. It was no longer making headlines in the secular press. Some thought that the NFPC was retrenching. Others judged that it was entering into mature relationships with the bishops. Sociologists might think that the Federation was experiencing a 'routinization of charisma'. Other analysts, however, might say that it was simply changing directions. All these perspectives have some measure of truth. The NFPC has left behind a confrontation approach to the bishops. What are some of the implications of these changes for the NFPC as it moves into the future?

THE SERIOUS SEVENTIES

Conflict and change are as much a part of society as stability and harmony. Individuals and organizations dissent from inhuman and outmoded structures. With new vistas and normative arrangements, they attempt to replace rigid beliefs and embedded rules and sanctions.

Social movements are organizational phenomena involving ideologies, action, demands, and change (see Gusfield, 1970; Evans, 1973). A movement consists of attitudes about what is wrong with society. By collective action it advocates change, demanding reform from the establishment. The pressure for reform or call to revolution reflect the frustration and discontent of some segment of society. But who and why the discontent in America in the 1960s!

Post-war America experienced a revolution of affluency. Everyone, so most of our leaders thought, was content because they lived in a land of freedom where material well-being was just a matter of hard work. Then came the Montgomery bus boycott of 1956 and the civil rights movement began. Harrington discovered the forgotten poor and the welfare movement started. With the so-called 'generation gap', a youth movement began. The Vietnam war spawned the peace movement. Women were being treated shabbily; the result was the liberation movement. The church renewal movement started with the NFPC as one of its organizational manifestations. These movements of the 1960s have continued into the 1970s somewhat altered. For instance, the civil rights movement developed into racial nationalism, which later broadened to include Native Americans, the Spanish speaking, and European ethnics. A segment of the youth movement, converting itself into the Jesus movement, began seeking an interiorization of the spirit against the din of demonstrations. Middle-class altruists began to leave the movements of the underclass and formed environmental and consumer movements.

These movements centered on discontents resulting from the violation of human dignity, including the institutional denial of human rights of 'life, liberty, and pursuit of happiness'. Discrimination against the races and oppression against the poor had become so institutionalized that their patterns are almost invisible. This violation also included the denial of self-determination. In a democracy, government by and for the people is the ideal, but governmental and corporate bureacracies crushed out the notion of self-actualizing communities. The 1960s saw all sorts of people, for all sorts of reasons, rise up in anger. They were not a hopeless mass, but people with talent and time to challenge the structures of inequalities.

But the enthusiasm and drama of these movements have subsided. There is activity, serious activity, but it localized in certain institutional sectors of civic life. But the activity no longer commands the mass involvement of peoples affected. There are numerous reasons accounting for the subsiding of the various civil rights movements. Victories have been won, thus the 'problems' seemed to be solved in the eyes of many. Conflict and controversy takes its toll of energy and dedication. Many leaders are worn out with the years of turmoil. Other overriding issues such as inflation, recession, unemployment, and energy shortages have taken over the limelight. In the middle seventies, minorities are experiencing downward mobility and the attendant despair. College students are seeking careers not causes. The middle class are fighting inflation not inequality. The concentration of power and regulation of life by economic and political corporate giants have left many citizens powerless and inert. The sanctions and demands of the 'third' and 'fourth' worlds are altering our economic structures, policies, and life styles. The NFPC with its emphasis on 'value' issues of the common good will face the obstinacy of the serious seventies.

The NFPC, as part of the renewal movement, has challenged the hierarchy for about the same reasons that the secular movements protested against the establishments of society. It has fought for the rights of priests and has pressed for self-determination and shared leadership.

The fate of the NFPC depends a great deal on the contingenices and conditions of history. I have looked at the NFPC from a natural history perspective, showing how it has developed through several career stages. Some sociologists have a propensity to show how movements start with a clamor of enthusiasm, set up an agenda of goals, score early victories, arrive at a plateau, and finally devote their energies toward self-perpetuation.

This coming of power and its effective mobilization of course requires some stabilization. A movement must become institutionalized if it is going for the 'long haul'. It is in this process that danger lurks. Formalization often leads to the glorification of the organization itself. Leaders then become maintainence men wary of doing anything significant, which usually means controversial, for fear of losing the organization's status gains and legitimacy. The paradox is simply one in which its successes often become an obstacle to its original spirit.

As a movement continues to grow, it becomes susceptible to the pressures of change from its relevant environments. These changes produce new problems for the organizational requirements of internal and external adaptations, especially for the procurement and utilization of effec've leadership. Events of history and shifts in societal currents may critically influence its authenticity and present a severe crisis to its policy and direction. The question of how to remain true to itself will always haunt the leadership.

Another set of problems deals with the internal consolidation of an organization or movement. Both failures and successes may destroy the solidarity of a movement. The effort to find new and relevant goals and to establish their priorities may create divisions and factions over how changes should be handled (Gusfield, 1970: 498–500).

The kind of solidarity and unity a change-oriented organization requires is one of creative tension, mature dissent, and functional conflict. Without a structural complementarity, an organization faces stagnation and sterility. A successful organization must institutionalize challenges to itself to insure its innovative spirit.

The NFPC has had the genius to maintain a divergent leadership which promoted stability and change. Although there have been attempts by the Federation to throw out the associations, the leadership had defeated such moves. The uncomfortable company of senates and associations has been a small price to pay for maintaining creative leadership, but there are signs that things are changing in the NFPC environment, presenting it with a dangerous dilemma.

After the San Francisco convention, the NFPC entered a 'new era' of growth. It has been successful in affiliating more councils, most of which are senates, and none of which are associations. More importantly, many of the affiliated associations have been gradually losing the zest and urgency they once had. Some are even folding. Without this more liberal perspective, the NFPC is in danger of losing the much needed complementarity which insures a vital leadership.

What must the NFPC do to keep itself vibrant and avoid the pitfalls of formalization and self-perpetuation? It would be wise, organizationally speaking, for the NFPC to maintain its 'unofficial' status *vis-à-vis* the NCCB. To push for and receive official recognition would make it much more susceptible to control. To combat formalization and promote flexibility, the NFPC should strengthen its structural dialectic of senate and association memberships. It might consider a new mechanism such as a pre-convention caucus day in which the House of Delegates would be separated into two chambers representing the senates and associations. This would provide a sharper focus on the kinds of rationales for or against resolutions to be debated before the full House.

The NFPC should strengthen its provincial structures and regional meetings to insure democratic representation and provide opportunities for the percolation of fresh ideas and new approaches from the rank and file. Periodically the NFPC should be punctuated with charismatic leaders in the top offices. This would renew the original purposes of the Federation, providing it with a certain sense of destiny.

Probably the most important thing the NFPC must do is to

continue 'to know the territory'. It must analyze conditions, climate, and trends within both the church and the world.

If any word could summarize the climate in the church and in the world, it is powerlessness. People, not just the lower classes but all segments of society, feel alienated from their leaders. Recent polls have shown a tremendous drop of confidence in our major institutions. O'Brien (1974: 5), in an address to the 1974 House of Delegates, stated:

> The sense of powerlessness so broadly present in our society ... pervades the Churches, as well, producing the phenomenon of intense personal religious experience amid the gradual disintegration of Church programs and Church structures. Who among us has recently met a really enthusiastic exponent of renewal in the American Church? Where does one find that excited militancy that characterized the early days of such groups as the National Association of Laymen or the National Federation of Priests' Councils?

O'Brien went on to say that concentrated power in society, whether exercised by corporate or ecclesiastical bureaucracies, will pervert the political process and destroy the foundations of democracy. Active participation in the life of the Church is necessary to make social life truly human (O'Brien, 1974: 18–19). Shaw (1973) sees the root of alienation of American Catholics in a secular value system which has become dominant. The Supreme Court has institutionalized these values in its decisions on abortion and public assistance to parochial schools. The abortion decision reflects a utilitarian approach to human life, while school aid involves the question of whether American Catholics will be accepted on their own terms or the dominant society will define what terms are acceptable.

This sense of powerlessness has affected bishops, priests, religious, and laity alike. But the alienation is not total. While bishops are in a quandary not only in regard to the Supreme Court and wholesale political corruption, but also in regard to the Vatican, they are beginning to show some courage, independence, and initiative. The NCCB voted to reverse the Vatican decision to end experimental procedures regarding marriages and annulments and voted to express concern to the Vatican regarding the norm of confession before communion (Casey, 1973: 1). Perhaps the recent mission of the NCCB to Rome in regard to these questions, as well as the initiation of the 'Campaign for Human Development', which funds social action projects, bodes well for a new kind of leadership.

As middle managers of the Church, priests have felt the sense of marginality more than any other sector of the Catholic Church. It is small wonder that nearly 14,000 priests *officially* resigned from the ministry between 1964 and 1970 (O'Grady, 1972: 3). Other adaptations to alienation by priests have been assignment relocation and passivity (Seidler, 1974). Those most likely to leave the ministry are associate pastors who have no powers except those which are delegated. Loyalty to the priesthood is strongest in religious orders. One reason for this is that they elect their superiors for set periods of time (see Greeley, 1974). This points to the need for continuing the trend of democraticizing the Church.

But another response has been one of mobilization. The clergy, brothers, laity, sisters, and seminarians have organized themselves in numerous ways to bring about change. They are changing their ministry in response to new societal trends. The Catholic Committee for Urban Ministry is responding to the institutionalized repression of ghetto life. The Catholic Conference on Urban Ethnic Affairs is ministering to the 'new pluralism' in American society. The Padres and Black Clergy Caucus are listening to the voices of cultural pluralism. The revitalized National Catholic Conference on Interracial Justice will concentrate on fighting injustices faced by blue collar workers. The Church's involvement in recent community organizations is also with these middle income groups. These newer ministerial approaches are addressing a new trend of an 'urban populism'. It is a trend that needs careful analysis because the interests of working-class ethnics and racial nationalism of the lower classes have the potential for either a new kind of urban protest or coalition.

Another trend is the tremendous impact of women religious. They are at the forefront of ministerial experimentation, serving as assistant pastors, preaching, and counselling. They are no longer cloistered in the convent, but involved in the totality of society, such as service in public schools, education for prisoners, rehabilitation of drug addicts, political lobbying, and community organization. This trend will continue to mount pressure for ordination of women and equal status with men in governing the Church.

Even the Catholic charismatics, whose emphasis has been on the interiorization of the Spirit, healing, and reconciliation, are beginning a thrust toward social action (Castelli, 1974).

Another important trend is the marked decrease in polarization in the Church. In the nearly ten years since the close of Vatican II, the Catholic Church experienced divisions of crisis proportions. Many of the changes demanded by the liberal segment of the Church are now accomplished. Democracy, representation, consultation, and even shared governance have increasingly become a norm in such structures as diocesan and parish pastoral councils, Catholic school boards, diocesan senates, and personnel boards. Bishops have been more willing to both share their authority and to exercise progressive leadership.

While there are still unmet challenges, especially in renewing the world with justice and peace, the accomplishments within the Church have presented problems for some of the more liberal organizations. They are experiencing, on one hand, a loss of purpose and an agenda for action. On the other hand, a large number of the liberal segment have become either apathetic or have left the Church. This factor has also contributed to the 'sense of calm' in the Church. The polarization which still remains in the Church has shifted from liberals confronting the once conservative hierarchy to conservatives, especially among the laity, attacking the church leadership on matters of progressive religious education and liberal views regarding social issues.

The rise of vocal conservatives is an important development within the Church. These traditionalists are concerned that too many liberals are moving into control of the chanceries, seminaries, and parochial education. They are also upset with the growth of 'unorthodox' theology creeping into religious textbooks and the increasing relativity of Catholic morality, such as homosexuality, remarriage for divorced Catholics, and abortion. Though small in number, they command a great amount of influence by the fact that they control to a large extent the national Catholic press (see *Time*, 1974). This trend will have a great impact on the renewal process, perhaps causing a polarization of larger proportions.

I have sampled just a few trends in the Church and society which will influence the future course of the NFPC. To maintain its effectiveness the NFPC will need to continually inform itself of the implications of such trends for the ministry.

The most important job the NFPC has is to develop replacement models for old traditions and values. Relying on the strengths of democratic participation, group leadership, dialectical unity, inter-organizational cooperation, and 'think tank' activities, it can carry forth the servanthood of Christ, transforming the human condition. Doing this the NFPC will be a reason for hope . . . *Si, se puede!*

Appendices

Constitution National Federation
of Priests' Councils
March 21, 1973

PREAMBLE

We priests of the United States of America, of Western and Eastern Rites, united in our respective councils, cognizant of the spirit of co-responsibility expressed in the Second Vatican Council by which we share with the bishops the work of providing creatively for the pastoral care of the People of God, and cognizant of our responsibility with the whole Church of showing our concern for the entire community in which we live, and desiring to collaborate on a national level in the realization of these responsibilities, do hereby establish a federation of priests' councils for the United States of America.

ARTICLE I: NAME

The name of this organization shall be the National Federation of Priests' Councils. (NFPC)

ARTICLE II: PURPOSE

The purpose or purposes of the NFPC shall be religious and educational:

1. To promote priestly brotherhood by facilitating communication among priests' councils.
2. To provide a forum for the discussion of pastoral matters.
3. To enable priests' councils to speak with a common, representative voice.
4. To promote and collaborate in programs of pastoral research and action.
5. To implement norms for the renewal of priestly life.
6. To provide the means for priests' councils, united nationally, to cooperate with the laity, the religious, the bishops, and with others in addressing the needs of our church in the modern world.
7. To do whatever is necessary to carry out these purposes.

ARTICLE III: MEMBERSHIP

The member councils shall be those which meet the membership requirements stated in the By-Laws. (Chapter I, Section A.)

ARTICLE IV: HOUSE OF DELEGATES

The House of Delegates shall determine the policies of the NFPC and shall deliberate those matters recommended to it either by the Executive Board or by the delegates. Its decisions shall be binding on the Executive Board.

ARTICLE V: EXECUTIVE BOARD

The Executive Board shall carry out the will of the House of Delegates and take whatever other actions it judges to be necessary for achieving the purposes of the NFPC. It shall be accountable for its actions to the House of Delegates.

ARTICLE VI: MEETINGS

The Executive Board shall meet at least four times annually. There shall be a plenary meeting of the House of Delegates at least annually in the spring. Members of the House of Delegates shall meet additionally at least once a year on a regional basis. Plenary meetings of the House of Delegates shall be called by the Executive Board.

ARTICLE VII: OFFICERS

The president shall be elected by the House of Delegates and shall become ex officio a member of the Executive Board. In the event he is already a member of the Executive Board, his provincial seat shall be vacated and the affiliated councils from that province shall elect a substitute to serve in his stead on the Executive Board during the term of his presidency. The Executive Board shall elect from its own number a vice-president, secretary and treasurer.

Article VIII: Amendments

The House of Delegates may amend this constitution at any plenary meeting provided that the proposed amendment, signed by ten delegates, be in the possession of the Executive Board 40 days before that meeting, that it be mailed to the member councils 30 days before that meeting, and that a two-thirds majority of the House of Delegates seated at that meeting concur in the amendment.

Article IX: Dissolution and Use of Income

In the event of the liquidation or dissolution of the corporation, the assets remaining after all debts have been satisfied, shall be conveyed to a non-profit organization, qualified for tax exemption as defined by Sec. 501 (c) (3) of the Internal Revenue Code, to be used for purposes as nearly as practicable analogous to those for which this organization was established.

No part of the net income of the corporation (or other entity) shall insure to the benefit of any private individual; and no director, member, trustee, officer, employee or other person, shall receive, or be lawfully entitled to receive, any pecuniary benefit, profit or compensation of any kind therefrom, except reasonable compensation authorized in the By-Laws for services rendered, or expenses incurred, in effecting one or more of the purposes for which it had been established.

By-Laws

Membership Requirements

CHAPTER I

A. *Eligibility*
   1. Diocesan Senates of Priests are eligible for membership.
   2. Priests' Associations, in which membership is available to all the priests in the diocese whose membership rosters list not less than 10% of the diocesan (secular) priests are eligible. There may not be more than one Priests' Association from each diocese.
   3. Councils of Religious priests which comply with the general organizational principles of senates and associations are eligible.

4. Other councils of priests which have been approved for membership by 2/3 vote of the House of Delegates are eligible.
5. Priests as individuals are not eligible for membership.

B. *Affiliation.* In order to affiliate with the NFPC, a priests' council must submit a copy of its constitution or by-laws, written signification of its intent to affiliate, and payment of its initiation fee.

C. *Credentials.* The Executive Board, functioning as a Credentials Committee, shall review the membership requirements of all Councils desiring to affiliate with the NFPC. If there is a dispute about whether a priests' council meets with the requirements of Chapter I, Section A of the By-Laws, appeal may be made to the House of Delegates.

House of Delegates

CHAPTER II

A. *Composition.* The House of Delegates shall consist of those delegates elected by their respective member councils. The delegates, at the time of their election, must be members of the councils they represent.

B. *Term of office.* The term of office of a delegate shall be determined by the local council.

C. *Quorum.* One hundred delegates, representing not less than one half of the member councils, shall constitute a quorum for the transaction of business.

D. *Representation*
   1. Member councils will be entitled to send delegates to the plenary meetings of the House of Delegates according to the following scale:
      —one delegate for each council representing 100 priests or less;
      —two delegates for each council representing 101 to 500 priests;
      —three delegates for each council representing 501 to 1000 priests;
      —four delegates for each council representing more than 1000 priests.
   2. Diocesan Senates shall be considered as representing all the priests in the diocese. Associations shall be considered as representing only those priests who are members of the association. Councils of

religious order priests will be considered as representing only those priests who are members of the council.

3. Alternate delegates may be elected by the priests' councils.

E. *Voting.* Each duly registered delegate present at the House of Delegates meetings shall have one vote.

F. *Registration.* Before being seated at any plenary meetings of the House of Delegates, each delegate or his alternate shall deposit with the Credentials Committee a certificate signed by the president or secretary of the member council or by both stating that the delegate has been regularly elected to the House of Delegates.

G. *Rules of procedure.* Robert's Rules of Order Revised, as modified by whatever special rules of procedure may be adopted by the House of Delegates, shall obtain in plenary meetings in the House of Delegates.

Executive Board

CHAPTER III

A. *Composition*
   1. The Executive Board shall be composed of one representative from each of the ecclesiastical provinces in the United States. For the purpose of representation on the Executive Board, the province of Washington, D.C. shall be considered as part of the province of Baltimore and the province of Anchorage shall be considered as part of the province of Seattle. The Eastern Rite dioceses shall be collectively considered as one ecclesiastical province. Councils of Religious priests shall be considered as one ecclesiastical province.
   2. The Executive Board members shall be elected by the affiliated councils of each province.

B. *Term of office*
   1. Their term of office shall begin at the conclusion of the spring meeting which coincides with or follows their election and shall cease at the conclusion of the spring meeting two years later. They may not be elected consecutively to more than two terms. If the seat of a board member has been vacated, the member councils from the province shall elect someone to complete the term. If an interim appointee has not been elected within 40 days of the date

when the seat was vacated, the Executive Board may elect a delegate from the province to complete the term.

2. For the purpose of electing a representative to the Executive Board, the councils of Religious priests shall choose one member of the Executive Board.

C. *Quorum.* A simple majority shall constitute a quorum of the Executive Board.

D. *Steering committee.* The Executive Board shall elect from its own members a Steering Committee to work with the president. The Steering Committee will prepare the agenda for Executive Board meetings.

E. *Voting.* Each member of the Executive Board shall have one vote.

F. *Rules of procedure.* Rules of Procedure for meetings of the Executive Board shall be determined according to the Constitution and By-Laws of the NFPC and according to Robert's Rules of Order Revised.

Officers

CHAPTER IV

A. *Term of office*
1. The term of office of the president shall be two years. The term of office of the vice-president, secretary and treasurer shall be one year.
2. No officer may serve consecutively more than two terms in the same office.
3. The newly-elected president shall commence his term of office on the July 1 after his election. He shall attend as president-elect any Executive Board meetings held between his election and the commencement of his term on July 1. The other officers commence their term of office immediately upon accepting their election.

B. *Nominations.* The Executive Board shall present to the House of Delegates a list of nominees for the office of President.

C. *Duties*
1. The President shall preside at all meetings of the Executive Board and the Steering Committee.
2. The Vice-President shall perform the duties of the President in his absence.

3. The Secretary shall supervise the recording of the Minutes of the Executive Board.
4. The Treasurer shall be the custodian of the NFPC funds.

Committees

CHAPTER V

Committees shall be established by the Executive Board to work on those matters determined by the House of Delegates. Committee chairman shall be appointed by the Executive Board from its own membership. Committee members shall be selected by committee chairmen. Committees shall be directly accountable to the Executive Board.

Budget, Dues, and Fees

CHAPTER VI

A. The NFPC shall operate on a fiscal year basis, the fiscal year commencing July 1 and terminating June 30 of the following year.

B. The initiation fee for a council shall be one hundred dollars ($100.00) for each delegate representing that council in the House of Delegates.

C. The Executive Board shall be charged with preparing the annual budget, and it shall submit the budget to the House of Delegates. The House of Delegates shall have the power of approving, rejecting, amending or remanding the budget.

D. The member councils shall pay an annual assessment as determined by the Executive Board. Assessments shall be prorated to the annual budget. The basis for prorating the assessments shall be the number of priests represented by each member council. The Executive Board shall establish each year a maximum per capita assessment beyond which no member councils shall be assessed.

E. The annual assessments of the member councils shall be set on or before June 1 for the succeeding fiscal year and the member councils shall be immediately notified of the amount of the assessment required to be paid by them for the succeeding fiscal year. On the 1st day of July, the annual assessment shall be due and payable. The annual assessment may be paid in one lump sum or in quarterly payments during the fiscal year.

F. Suspension under these By-Laws shall mean that no member council suspended shall be permitted to vote on any matter before the NFPC nor shall any member council be permitted to have a voice in any of the business of the NFPC, nor shall any such suspended member council nor any of its members have the right to receive any materials, studies or work product prepared by the NFPC or under its auspices except as the Executive Board may otherwise determine.

G. In the event that any member council be delinquent two years in the payment of the assessment, than on the second anniversary of the date of the last payment of the assessment by said member council, the membership council, shall, without more, be terminated, and thereafter if said former member council shall again wish to become a member of the NFPC, it shall be subject to the provisions of Article III of the Constitution, and Chapter VI and Section B of this Chapter and these By-Laws.

H. It shall be within the power of the Executive Board upon recommendation of the Finance Committee to suspend the operation of Sections E, F and G of this Chapter of these By-Laws.

Ecclesiastical Provinces

CHAPTER VII

Atlanta, Baltimore/Washington, D.C., Boston, Chicago, Cincinnati, Denver, Detroit, Debuque, Eastern Rite, Hartford, Indianapolis, Kansas City, Los Angeles, Louisville, Miami, Milwaukee, Newark, New Orleans, New York, Oklahoma City, Omaha, Philadelphia, Portland, Religious Priests, St. Louis, St. Paul/Minneapolis, San Antonio, San Francisco, Santa Fe, Seattle/Anchorage.

Amendments

CHAPTER VIII

The House of Delegates may amend these By-Laws at any plenary meeting provided that the proposed amendment, signed by 10 delegates, be in the possession of the Executive Board, 40 days before the meeting, that it be mailed to the member councils 30 days before that meeting, and that a majority of the House of Delegates seated at that meeting concur in the amendment.

Theory and Methods
of Research

A Theoretical Perspective

INTRODUCTION

When people are asked to join an organization, invariably the question comes up about its worth. How good is it? What progress is it making? How solid is the organization? Such questions as these relate to the question of the organization's effectiveness or success. Some might say that the NFPC is a great success and has demonstrated its effectiveness by the mere fact that it continues to operate as an autonomous organization within the American Catholic Church. To not only survive but to assist in the accomplishment of such goals as the widespread adoption of diocesan due process machinery without having the official approval of the Catholic hierarchy is an impressive display of effectiveness. But effectiveness needs specification and precision for it to be a useful analytical tool.

I will develop a model of organizational effectiveness derived from the social system perspective and apply it to the National Federation of Priests' Councils. It asserts that effectiveness is related to a variety of organizational objectives, such as procurement of resources, collaboration, morale, and attainment of goals; hence, the definition of effectiveness is viewed as multi-dimensional. The discussion points to the need of establishing a benchmark to evaluate the growth and effectiveness of a single organization. This can be done by studying similar organizations or the same organization over time. I have chosen the latter approach.

AN ORGANIZATIONAL CAREER MODEL

An organization is a social entity composed of human groupings deliberately constructed and reconstructed to seek specific goals (Parsons, 1960: 17). As noted by Etzioni (1964: 3), organizations are characterized by (1) divisions of labor, power, and communication responsibilities; (2) the presence of one or more power centers which control the concerted efforts of the organization and direct these activities toward its goals; and (3) the capability of substituting its personnel.

Organizational requirements, according to Parsons (1959: 5–16), are related to the external organizational environment, on the one hand, and are concerned with the internal organizational means and ends on the other. An organization is established to attain certain external ends: *goal attainment.* Also, it must procure and employ certain means or resources to attain its external goals: *adaptation.* It must internally coordinate and adjust the autonomous units into a working order: *integration.* Finally, it must employ internal means to manage possible tensions and conflicts among the units: *tension management* (latency). These four functional requirements or needs must be successfully satisfied for an organization to maintain itself and survive. These organizational needs are related to a wide array of characteristics at any given phase of organizational development, involving both the internal and external functions of the system. Barton (1961: 1–2) classifies these characteristics as follows.

External Characteristics:
Inputs: procurement of personnel and material resources
Outputs: effects and consequences of organizational activity
Environment: its relations with the public or with other organizations

Internal Characteristics:
Social structure: formal and informal structures of communication and
    work coordination
Attitudes: individual states of mind concerning satisfaction, morale
    consensus, etc.
Activities: collective processes and decision-making mechanisms

These elements of the system must be procured, coordinated, and utilized with differential emphasis to be effective in solving the major internal and external functional needs of the organization at any given phase of existence.

An organization obviously must first be established. It then progresses from one stage of development to another, involving consolidation, ongoing operations, and modifications due to internal and external conditions (Caplow, 1964: 119–21). Thus, when viewed over time, a given organization has various stages or a sequence of organizational postures or positions.

A useful concept in developing a sequential model of various types of organizational behavior is that of *career.* This concept, originally developed in studies of occupations (Hughes, 1958: 56–57 and 102–15), refers to the sequence of movements from one position to another in an occupational system by any worker in that system. This notion also includes the concept of career contingency, namely, those factors, both structural and personal, on which the successful sequence from one position to another depends.

The career of an organization seems to involve a sequence of movements through several stages or classes of events. Certain contingencies must be sufficiently met and definite problems solved for the organization to effectively or successfully move to another stage of development. Within each stage the organization has an identifiable position determined by the events present at that stage. These events are the elements which provide the researcher with an organizational profile of structural and functional regularities. I identify four stages and their associated organizational patterns: (1) foundation, (2) consolidation, (3) operational, and (4) achievement of goals.

It is important to clarify one aspect of the career model of organizational effectiveness. I do not imply that the four stages of organizational development are fixed intervals. This is an empirical question. Moreover, there is not necessarily a unilinear development of organizational growth. For instance, it is quite possible for an organization to attain several objectives simultaneously. Once the organization is ongoing and is successfully attaining its goals, it may for a period of time have to devote more of its energy to reconsolidation. In this instance, the consolidation objectives will have the immediate primacy. In other words, within this proposed framework an investigator can study any of the organizational needs or objectives and their related aspect of effectiveness at any period of the organizational history.

The class of events in the foundation stage of the natural history of the organization involves the following patterns or regularities:

1. Recruitment of personnel and organizational skills.
2. Procurement of material resources.
3. Formulation of normative patterns: formal authority, work patterns, and communication structure.
4. Emerging processes of consensus and cohesion.

Adaptation functions have an instrumental character referring basically to the relation of the system to its external environment. The adaptation requirement is mainly a problem of acquiring all the human and material resources, such as entrepreneurial skills, which are necessary for the achievement of organizational goals. In the foundation stage, the organizational processes seem especially involved with the adaptation requirement. I call this sub-type of organizational effectiveness acquisition or procurement effectiveness. The solution of the initial adaptive problems is a necessary condition for a successful movement into the next stage.

In the consolidation stage, the processes at work are oriented toward the internal needs of the organization in order to develop a cooperative system in a beneficial working order (Selznick, 1948). The characteristics of these patterns are:

1. Patterns of cohesion or tension management.
2. Integrative patterns of consensus.
3. Functional integration or collaboration.
4. Communication integration.

During this phase of activity, the organization must concentrate its energy, resources, and talent on the maturation of its internal system. The paramount problems it must face and adequately solve are those of integration and tension management or cohesion. The more coordinated or integrated the structure and the more the members are attracted to and bound up with other members, the more effectively the organization will overcome barriers as it strives to realize its goals (Blau, 1964: 56–60).

Integration of the social system implies several dimensions, according to Landecker (1955). Normative integration or consensus is the degree of members' conformity and agreement to the organization's norms and values. Communicative integration is the degree of sufficiency of information exchanges transmitted through available channels of the organization. Functional integration is the degree to which there is a reciprocal exchange of tasks among the units of a system resulting in the interdependence or synchronization of these units. In defining organizational integration as the ability to maintain or increase the volume of interaction among its positions, Caplow (1964: 123) sees this functional characteristic as a significant measure of effectiveness. In sum, the organization must sufficiently solve its integrative problems in order to proceed effectively into full-fledged operations. Organizational effectiveness in the consolidation stage will be primarily related to this functional requirement, as well as to that of tension management. I now turn to this latter problem.

Latent tension management (cohesion) requirements refer to the internal processes which insure that the attraction and motivational commitment of the individual members to the organization are sufficiently adequate for the proper performance of the organizational tasks (Parsons, 1959: 5–11). This requirement implies that the organization is able to develop and to maintain a certain attractiveness in order to hold the loyalty and interests of the members, thus providing for adequate stability. In short, during the consolidation phase the organization must manifest a sufficient degree of cohesion.

Meeting this functional requirement is especially salient in the consolidation stage of an organizational career. If there is not sufficient satisfaction, motivation, and effort-reward balance above some minimum critical level at this stage, the organization may become incapacitated due to heavy strains and conflicts. Truman (1962: 112) recognizes the importance of cohesion for organizational effectiveness. He holds that the formal organization itself is evidence of a considerable degree of cohesion because it is indicative of a high frequency of interaction, shared values, expectation of stability, acceptance or legitimation of the leadership, and the allocation of tasks and policy directives.

To summarize, an organization must focus its activities and resources inward in order to meet the requirements of consensus, communication, collaboration, and cohesion. This phase, primarily devoted to meeting these problems or accomplishing these objectives, has been described as the consolidation stage. I have noted the crucial nature of these functions. The second sub-type of organizational effectiveness can be defined in terms of meeting these requirements. I call this consolidation effectiveness. By now it should be clear that organizational effectiveness must be viewed as a multi-dimensional phenomenon. It is important to point out that once an organization attains its major objectives, such as procurement of material and human resources at the foundation stage, it cannot assume that it will be effective in these same activities at a later stage. In short, as an organization such as the NFPC grows and passes through several critical stages, it has to be effective in meeting more requirements so that it can continue to survive and to produce outputs in line with its general goals and values. There is, then, a crescive development, both qualitatively and quantitatively speaking, of organizational demands which require larger amounts of resources, more efficient utilization of skills, and greater consolidation of all aspects of the system in achieving its goals.

The four functional needs converge during the operational and goal-attainment phases. These two stages are difficult to distinguish empirically although they are analytically distinct. The operational stage has to do with the mobilization and coordination of all the resources of the system for the accomplishment of the organizational goals. The system employs the adaptive processes not only for continual procurement of different kinds of resources, but also for the solution of problems that may act as barriers to the goal-attainment processes. The organization must maintain its consensual, communicative, functionally integrative, and cohesive patterns to manage intra-organizational conflicts.

During the operational stage, however, the organization is basically concerned with the problem of fitting the proper means to desired ends; and meeting the internal adaptative requirements seems to be paramount at this stage. It is in this phase that the decision-making processes become prominent. The problem of material and human resource utilization, maintenance of the internal system in working order, and all the decisions which these elements necessitate are the problems of organizational power or control.

Parsons (1956: 228) defines power as the 'capacity to mobilize resources in the interest of the attainment of a system goal'. The decision-making processes in the operational stage are thus related to all the functional requirements of the system. For instance, technical decisions are partially related to the adaptive problem of procuring and utilizing resources. Managerial decisions imply the problems of integration and cohesion. Policy decisions establish and specify the characteristics of particular goals of the organization based on the estimate of both the power of the system and the environmental conditions. In this stage of progress toward certain goals, organizational effectiveness can best be viewed in terms of a power objective. This objective is related to the internal adaptation function. I call this third sub-type power effectiveness.

Organizations are established for particular purposes which we call the goals of the organization. The 'real' goals of the organization, in contrast to the stated goals, are those desired states towards which the majority of the means of the organization and the major commitments of its members are directed. Some authors, as previously noted, have defined organizational effectiveness in terms of the degree to which goals, be they formal or derived, are realized. Although measuring organizational effectiveness exclusively in terms of the degree of goal attainment does not provide an overall picture of organizational effectiveness, it does, however, provide one important dimension of success, namely, goal-attainment effectiveness. In assessing this fourth sub-type of effectiveness, it is important to determine the actual goals of the organization together with their priorities. By doing this, research can determine any crucial relationships between goal priority and effectiveness.

A Definition Organizational Effectiveness

I have argued that an organization has a certain natural history in which it moves through different phases of development. I have also argued that the organization must meet four functional requirements in order to maintain itself and to achieve its goals. Organizational effectiveness can thus be framed in terms of objectives derived from these requirements. I call these objectives: (1) acquisition, (2) consolidation, (3) power, and (4) goal attainment. Thus, I define effectiveness as the extent to which an organization attains its acquisition, consolidation, power, and goal objectives.

In summary, these four categories of objectives constitute a scheme which serves to arrange a discussion of the separate dimensions into a coherent framework. This affords one a tool of analysis to explore and to identify the significant elements and processes that contribute to this or that form of organizational effectiveness and to generate explanatory hypotheses about the causes of the effectiveness syndrome at different stages of organizational development. The criteria of the system model allow me to obtain a comparative profile of effectiveness of the NFPC from 1969 to 1972. See Figure B.1 for a system effectiveness model.

I am particularly interested in how effectiveness varies over time, in terms of both consolidation processes and operative goals. I have specified consolidation effectiveness as a sub-model of organizational effectiveness in terms of organizational consensus, cohesion, communicative integration, and collaboration. Consolidation effectiveness is defined as the extent to which an organization successfully attains these above-mentioned objectives (see Figure B.2).

Goal effectiveness is defined as the extent to which an organization successfully realizes the operative goals of the organization. Many organizations have multiple goals. Some are intermediate goals which are necessary conditions for attaining ultimate goals. In other words, there is differential progress or effectiveness based on such factors as goal priorities, temporal stages, and leadership orientations (Seashore, 1965: 26–30). For instance, some organizational leaders who are more 'value'- than 'interest'-oriented may put greater emphasis on commonweal goals and evaluate effectiveness accordingly. I will now discuss the research strategy.

Figure B.1   *A system effectiveness model*

Career stages	Functional requirements	Objectives	Effectiveness
Foundation	Adaptation (external)	*Acquisition	*Acquisition
	Adaptation (internal)	*Consolidation	*Consolidation
	Integration and latency		
Consolidation	Integration and latency (cohesion)	*Consolidation	*Consolidation
	Adaptation		
	Goal Attainment		
Operation ⎫ Performance	Adaptation (external)		
	Adaptation (internal)	*Power	*Power
	Integration and latency (cohesion)		
	Goal attainment	*Goal attainment	*Goal attainment
Attainment ⎭	Goal attainment	*Goal attainment	*Goal attainment
	Adaptation (external)		
	Adaptation (internal)	*Power	*Power
	Integration and latency (cohesion)		

* Dominant (theoretically speaking).

Figure B.2   *A model of consolidation effectiveness*

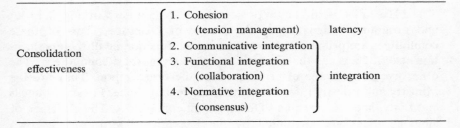

Methods of Research

INTRODUCTION

From its beginning, the NFPC has been an organizational paradox. While the majority of its affiliates were ecclesiastically approved senates, the Federation itself has never sought or received episcopal approval. Formally, and in the eyes of many bishops, it has been an illegitimate organization posing a threat to hierarchical authority.

I will describe the structural characteristics of the NFPC as well as the research strategy of the study, including a discussion of data collection techniques and sources of data.

The Federation is presently composed of 121 affiliated councils. The affiliates are mainly diocesan senates and free associations with some religious order councils.

ORGANIZATIONAL STRUCTURE OF NFPC

The formal structure of the NFPC consists of the following units: there are four officers, an executive board, a policy body called the 'House of Delegates', and the affiliated councils.

The Executive Board presently consists of twenty-eight members representing the twenty-eight provinces in the USA. The Executive Board members are elected by the council delegates from their respective provinces. The function of this board is to carry out the will of the House of Delegates and to take whatever other actions it judges as necessary for achieving the goals of the NFPC. It is, however, accountable for its actions to the House of Delegates. This Executive Board meets at least four times each year.

The Executive Board has at present seven committees working on issues and programs designated by the House of Delegates. Two of these committees are primarily concerned with the functioning of the organization itself. They are the Finance and Communication committees. The other five concern the external goals of the organization. They are the Ministry and Priestly Life, Personnel, Justice and Peace, Priests' Councils and Laity, and Research and Development committees. The chairmen of all committees are appointed by the Executive Board from its own membership.

The policy body of the NFPC is the House of Delegates. The number of priests represented by the council determines the number of delegates from any given council. Delegates are elected for a two-year term. The size of the House of Delegates varies with the number of affiliates. In 1968, 114 councils affiliated with the newly formed organization. By October, 1975, there were 121 affiliates. The delegates are elected by the member councils and are usually council officers. The ultimate power of the NFPC in determining policy lies with this body. It meets annually at a national convention to formulate policy for the organization.

To better facilitate communication exchanges concerning the direction of the NFPC, there is also a provincial structure consisting of a member of the Executive Board and the presidents and officers of the local councils which are located in the geographical boundary of the provincial jurisdiction. Most of these provincial structures do not define themselves as official entities of the NFPC. As one goes from the national to the local level, less and less do priests associate activities related to the NFPC with the NFPC. This is perhaps due to the bishops' negative attitude toward the national organization. The twenty-nine provinces meet annually to discuss the problems of the local councils, to exchange information concerning councils' procedures and programs, and to assist in the formulation of the agenda of the national meeting of the NFPC. In terms of organizational structure, the provinces are presently in varying degrees of development. See Figure B.3 for the organizational chart of the NFPC.

RESEARCH STRATEGY

The focus of the study is the organizational development and effectiveness of the NFPC. Explicit in this strategy is the investigation of the organizational characteristics and purposes of the NFPC since its inception. I have

Figure B.3 *The Organizational Chart for the NFP* (Taken from *NFPC Newsletter,* I(1), July 1968, but adapted and updated as of January 1, 1976)

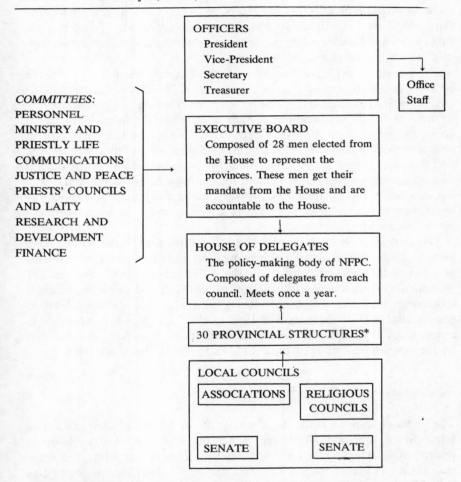

Senates represent all the priests of the diocese. Associations and other groups represent only their members. There is only one association per diocese, and its rosters must list at least 20% of diocesan (secular) priests.

* There are 30 provinces in the United States; however, only 28 are represented on the executive board, plus one religious order province.

employed both historical and sociological analysis whenever appropriate to the nature of the topic. Although I concern myself about the how and why the NFPC started, I am primarily interested in the following two questions: How worthwhile or effective has the NFPC been since its establishment? And what have been its major concerns and policy trends? To answer the first question I have developed a career model of organizational effectiveness which I have just discussed.

The period of organizational development covers the period from the NFPC's establishment to the beginning of 1976. The foundation stage covers the period from the national feasibility meeting in February, 1968, to the first annual convention one year later, while the other three stages cover the years from 1969 through 1975. These first two years are of critical importance to the NFPC and the Catholic community. 1969 was the first complete year of NFPC operations. It was earmarked by confrontation and tensions between the NFPC and the Catholic bishops. The year 1972 began a new trend for the NFPC. It was a move away from bishops-clergy controversies about priests' rights and status, and a move toward the 'value' issues of social justice.

The second question deals with the policy directions of the NFPC, past, present, and future. This area of investigation takes up the major problems and issues that are of concern to the NFPC. These policy trends are identified by researching a wide variety of the NFPC's documents. Chapter 6 discusses the issues and trends during the foundation and consolidation phases, that is, from the period of 1968 to 1972. Chapter 7 discusses these trends from 1972 to the beginning of 1976. These directions are specified by the operational goals of the NFPC as found in the resolutions.

DESCRIPTION OF THE POPULATION STUDIED

The focus of analysis is the membership of the House of Delegates. The selection of this population represents the outcome of a number of interrelated factors. The following relevant factors constitute the most important considerations. (1) The strategic locus of the delegates embodies the ultimate authority of the organization. (2) It represents the best cross section of the organization in terms of both functional importance and manageable size. (3) Lastly, this unit is considered as more representative than any other unit for an investigation into different aspects of organizational effectiveness. For instance, over seventy-five percent of the delegates are also officers in their local councils. These positions provide them with a great deal of grassroots knowledge and interaction. They are also linked with the Executive Board insofar as the Board is elected from the membership of the House of Delegates. This strategy interlocking process of the national structure via the House of Delegates is considered the best available empirical referent to study the organizational processes of the NFPC.

TYPES AND SOURCES OF DATA AND COLLECTION TECHNIQUES

Data employed in this research project came from three questionnaires, personal interviews, participant observation, analyses of a wide variety of NFPC documents, Catholic and secular journals, and library research. Library resources and interviews were used to gather data on the climate of the priesthood as described in Chapter 1. Data resources for the historical analysis of the beginnings of the NFPC, found in Chapter 2, were the files of Father John Hill, one of the major architects of the NFPC; the Catholic and secular press were also analyzed for this period.

Materials employed in the description and analysis of NFPC's development and effectiveness were the proceedings of the national feasibility meeting in February, 1968; the constitutional meeting in May, 1968; and the proceedings of seven annual conventions. I analyzed the Executive Board's minutes; the President's Newsletter; and the NFPC's journal, *Priests' Forum*, and *Priests-USA* for the years 1968 through 1975. Personal interviews of leaders were also conducted. I administered questionnaires to the 1969 and 1972 delegates. The first questionnaire (Time One) was mailed to the 1969 delegates in November, 1969. Ninety percent of the questionnaires were returned, yielding data on 201 delegates out of 224 in the population. The same questionnaire (Time Two) was administered to the delegates in March, 1972, yielding a return of 89% and representing 186 respondents out of the total population of 208 delegates. The return rate of usable questionnaires in both studies is considered quite adequate to characterize the delegate population for each period. Another questionnaire, more narrow in focus, was administered to the New Orleans' delegates in March, 1969. There was a 69 percent return.

The main questionnaire consisted of two parts. The first part provides background data on the delegates, such as age, education, and position. The second part of the questionnaire contained items dealing with the four effectiveness dimensions (see the questionnaire items in Appendix E).

For analyzing the policy trends and issues (Chapters 6 and 7) I have relied solely on NFPC documents. The following were the main sources of data: (1) proceedings of all the national conventions; (2) the President's 'State of the Federation' message; (3) Executive Board minutes; (4) the NFPC's journals and newsletters, *Priests' Forum* and *Priests-USA:* (5) annual resolutions adopted; and (6) the *President's Newsletter.*

CLASSIFICATION OF VARIABLES

The variables used in the empirical approach are social-psychological in nature. They are derived from a questionnaire specially designed for this research task. The variables refer to a number of organizational processes and interpersonal relationships within the organization as perceived or judged by the respondents.

The variables are listed in Figure B.4 below. It should be noted that the variables employed here refer to several aspects of an organization which have been the focus of attention of students of organizations during the past two decades. Communication, cohesion, and functional interdependence have been employed by Likert (1961) at the University of Michigan. The consensus variables have been utilized by Georgopoulos (1957).

In summary, the scope of this study is to give a historical and sociological analysis of the origin and development of the NFPC within the framework of organizational effectiveness.

Figure B.4   *Variables employed in the survey*

Acquisition Variables

1. Number and percentage of affiliates
2. Recruitment of personnel and skill resources
3. Finance resources
4. Emerging patterns of organizational integration

Consolidation Variables

Cohesion

1. Sense of identity
2. Involvement
3. Satisfaction with organizational progress
4. General dissatisfaction (absence of)
5. Commitment to the organization
6. Organizational harmony

7. Friendliness among members

8. Absence of strains and conflict

Consensus

1. Regarding norms and beliefs

2. Regarding the objectives of the organization

3. Regarding the activities of the organization

4. Regarding the authority of the organization

5. Regarding the performance of the organization

6. Regarding the decisions of the organization

7. Agreement on the importance of the organization

Functional Integration

1. Structural adequacy

2. Established routines

3. Cooperation

4. Avoidance of interference

5. Efficient fulfillment of tasks

6. Mutual working relations

7. Smooth organizational operations

Communicative Integration

1. Adequacy of communication

2. Downward/upward communication

3. Helpfulness of communication

4. Strains re: communicative coordination

Power Mobilization

1. Influence of the NFPC on external organizations

2. Influences by others on the NFPC

3. Influence areas of the NFPC

4. Democratic decision-making processes

Goal Attainment

1. Specification of goals

2. Priority of goals

3. Progress toward goals

C

The Moment of Truth
NFPC Statement on the Priesthood, 1971

The moment of truth has arrived for us, the delegates of the National Federation of Priests' Councils of the United States of America, and for those whom we represent. There may never be another moment like this within our lifetime. We now wish to speak of our hopes and our concerns, our faith and our lives, within the Church and the world of today.

We address ourselves to the bishops of our country, to the bishops who will speak for us at the International Synod in Rome, and to the Synod itself.

We are men who live in a society marked by rapid and deep change. We are men who live in a Church in which 25,000 of our brother priests around the world have resigned in the past seven years. We are men who live in a Church where over one-third of the priests who participated in our survey, 'A Study of Priestly Celibacy', has a serious problem with the lack of leadership from those in authority and shares a deep disappointment in the Church's stand on social and moral issues. Almost one out of three of these priests surveyed is disturbed by the slow pace of change in view of the call for renewal by the bishops of Vatican II. Three out of four have one or more friends who have left the active ministry, and 25 % know others who plan to leave. We know that those who are leaving are, for the most part, creative and intelligent men.

The fact that life seems to be taking shape apart from the Church and without the gospel dimension disturbs a significant number of us. Many priests feel that they live in an isolated ecclesiastical world because of archaic Church structures. When we try to relate to this rapidly changing society we often merely react, arrive late on the scene, or imitate, but seldom lead.

The Church exists for the sake of the kingdom of God. It centers its life around people rather than institutional forms. The Church is the sign, the sacrament of the kingdom here on earth in our time, a dynamic movement within humanity, calling mankind to the kingdom which is to come.

The events of our time, therefore, demand that we speak. This, indeed, is our moment of truth.

LEADERSHIP

First, we speak to the problem which most seriously troubles priests today, the lack of leadership from those in authority, both bishops and priests.

Our ministerial priesthood reflects the love of Jesus Christ for his Church whenever bishops and priests are in dialogue and rapport. A bishop alone does not bear the responsibility for the ministry of the local Church. The bishop, along with his priests, religious and laity, shares this responsibility. Most difficulties arise from the refusal to share such responsibility.

We, therefore, call upon the bishops of the United States to share responsibilty on the local level. Such sharing must be initiated with mutual trust and genuine communication among bishops, priests, religious and laity. Vatican II states that the bishop should regard priests as his brothers and friends because they share in the same priesthood and ministry.

Effective leadership depends in large measure on the acceptance of the leader by the people. We, therefore, support the suggestions of the Canon Law Society of America for the selection of bishops which includes broad consultation with priests, reigious and laity. We also recommend a definite term of office for bishops.

CHURCH STRUCTURES

Church structures exist to serve the people of God. The basic structure through which most priestly ministry now operates is the geographic parish, with all that it implies in terms of residence, grouping of priest, life style, and patterns of authority. There is a place for such a structure, subject to necessary reform, but we are convinced that other forms are also necessary to meet the needs of the People of God in our times, and these new forms will grow from the needs they serve.

These needs may call for non-geographical apostolates, co-pastorates, self-supporting ministries, team approaches, and an expanded sharing in ministry by the laity, including an official ministry by women. Whatever their form, these ministries should not become mere individual solutions applied to existing problems. They must be part of a planned approach to Church re-organization. And in order to develop new ministries, priests must be given encouragement and financial assistance to design new programs, the freedom to experiment, and the opportunity to develop necessary skills.

HUMAN RIGHTS

Men question the honesty of a Church which is to be a model of justice and love, but which has often failed to protect among its own members those human rights which it holds up to the world as sacred. Therefore, we are compelled to demand that the human rights of all in the Church be secured through the immediate establishment of effective administrative tribunals and due process at every level in the Church.

We accept a corresponding responsibility on our part to recognize that all men have these same rights. We also insist on complete openness and accountability from all who serve the Church in any of its institutional structures.

CELIBACY

Celibacy is a precious tradition of the Church and must be preserved. Its witness value is an established fact. However, we are convinced that this value will be enhanced by being freely embraced and not as a necessary adjunct to the priesthood.

The substance of fidelity in ministry, however, is a commitment to service, and the charism of celibacy is subordinate to the charism of service. Faithful ministry in the Church can also be effectively exercised by married priests. Therefore, we are convinced that the present law of mandatory celibacy in the western Church must be changed.

Although such a change will involve certain practical difficulties and problems, the need for this change far outweighs the problems it might create, and we call for the change to begin now.

We ask that the choice between celibacy and marriage for priests now active in the ministry be allowed and that the change begin immediately. Furthermore, no group should be deprived of priests simply because married men cannot leave their families or environment to spend long years in formal seminary training. We ask that national hierarchies be empowered to implement plans at once which will allow the acceptance of married men as candidates for the priesthood. Finally, in a spirit of brotherhood, we ask that priests who have already married be invited to resume the active ministry. Decisions concerning the return of these men should be made by the Ordinary, the Personnel Board, the local community, and the priest himself in the light of particular circumstances.

Priests and Holiness

We affirm that the core of renewal lies in a change of heart, in an interior renewal for each priest. Nothing can so enrich the priest's interior life as knowing Jesus Christ crucified and risen. The priest's commitment is to bear witness to Christ no matter what form his ministry takes. He must be a man who knows Christ in the Eucharist and in the other sacraments, in the sacred Scriptures, in prayer, in the signs of the times, in the daily lives of people and in himself.

Jesus dedicated his life in service to his fellow man. The ordained minister of today and tomorrow, as a disciple of Jesus, can neither narrow his horizons of concern nor spurn the collaboration of others in the pursuit of rights and happiness for all mankind. The total ministerial resources of the Church can contribute much to meeting the social challenges of our day, especially in seeking peace, in easing social and racial tensions, in relieving poverty and sickness, in struggling for a sound ecology and in assisting underdeveloped and emerging nations.

The unique call to the priests of our times is to struggle as leaders for the renewal of society and the Church, and it is within this context of struggle that the priest develops his spirituality. We call for the rededication of priests to the mission of the Church today and for the reform of institutions within it, a reform which provides a climate of freedom to hear the call of the Spirit.

Conclusion

Change in our society is inevitable, and the Church must not fail to read the signs of the times. The renewal we call for is in accord with the best traditions of the Church, and reflects the thinking of the men and women who have committed their lives to the Church of Christ.

We speak to meet the needs of the people we serve, the culture we live in, and the call of the Spirit we follow. What we call for involves risk and courage, qualities that have marked Christians through the ages.

We call upon the National Conference of Catholic Bishops, the United States bishop-delegates to the International Synod of Bishops, and the Synod itself to support decisive legislation to initiate or implement our recommendations. We likewise invite all lay people, religious, deacons, priests and bishops to cooperate with one another in order to secure the objectives of these renewal proposals.

Without panic or despair, with realism and hope, we underscore the urgency of these recommendations. In the words of Ecclesiastes, 'There is an appointed time for everything . . . a time to tear down and a time to build . . . a time to keep and a time to cast away . . . a time to be silent and a time to speak . . .'. We would say a time for renewal, the moment of truth.

That moment is now!

D

Summary Tables

Summary Table. *Resolutions passed at NFPC annual conventions*

	1969 N=32	1970 N=48	1971 N=31	1969–71 N=111	1972 N=62	1973 N=23	1974 N=24	1972–74 N=109
JUSTICE AND PEACE								
1. Civil Rights re:	**8**	**4**	**15**	**27**	**13**	**13**	**10**	**36**
A. Racial justice principles; racial conflict, promote project equality; discriminatory clubs; immigration laws; homosexuals' civil rights	1	0	1	2	2	2	3	7
B. Death penalty; prison reform	1		1	2	1	1	2	4
2. Economic Justice re:	3	3	4	10	5	6	2	13
A. Reform, expansion of services to the poor e.g., guaranteed income; OEO; housing	1			1	2	1		3
B. Religious, financial, and legislative initiatives re: the poor	1	1	1	3	1	2		3
C. Support of economic movements for justice e.g., UFWA; AMOS; corporate responsibility	1	2	3	6	2	3	1	6
D. Roll back in fuel prices				0			1	1

Summary Table. *Resolutions passed at NFPC annual conventions (Continued)*

	1969 N=32	1970 N=48	1971 N=31	1969–71 N=111	1972 N=62	1973 N=23	1974 N=24	1972–74 N=109
JUSTICE AND PEACE (continued)								
3. War and Peace	2	0	8	10	4	3	2	9
A. Issues relating to conscientious objection, draft laws, and amnesty	1		2	3	2	2	1	5
B. Support of Berrigan brothers			2	2	1			1
C. Condemnation of South East Asia War; call for cease-fire			3	3	1			1
D. Opposition to build-up of military hardware	1		1	2		1	1	2
4. *International Justice re:*	0	0	2	2	2	1	1	4
A. Solidarity and involvement with oppressed peoples in Latin America			1	1	1	1	1	3
B. Free migration of Soviet Jews			1	1				0
C. Evils of colonialism			0	0	1			1
5. *Political Justice re:*	0	0	0	0	0	1	2	3
A. Justice at Wounded Knee				0		1		1
B. Favoring impeachment of president				0			1	1
C. Application of ethical standards in government				0			1	1

Summary Table. *Resolutions passed at NFPC annual conventions* (continued)

	1969 N=32	1970 N=48	1971 N=31	1969–71 N=111	1972 N=62	1973 N=32	1974 N=24	1972–74 N=109
JUSTICE AND PEACE (continued)								
6. *Community Organization and Needs*	2	1	0	3	0	0	0	0
A. Allotment of parish income to community needs	1			1				0
B. Train community organizers	1			1				0
C. Urge affiliation with IFCO		1		1				0
MINISTRY AND PRIESTLY LIFE	**11**	**13**	**5**	**29**	**14**	**6**	**8**	**28**
1. *Normative Interests of Priests re:*	9	9	4	22	3	3	1	7
A. Due process	3	5		8				0
B. Laicization process and its consequences	2		3	5	1	1	1	3
C. Optional celibacy	2	4		6	1	1		2
D. Reform of canon law	1			1				0
E. Study of theology and spirituality of the priesthood	1		1	2				0
F. Priests' life-style			1	0	1	1		2
2. *Ministerial Concerns*	0	3	0	3	5	1	6	12
A. Support of the Dutch Church		3		3				0
B. Ministry to homosexuals				0	1		1	2

Summary Table. *Resolutions passed at NFPC annual conventions (continued)*

	1969 N=32	1970 N=48	1971 N=31	1969-71 N=111	1972 N=62	1973 N=23	1974 N=24	1972-74 N=109
MINISTRY AND PRIESTLY LIFE (continued)								
2. Ministerial concerns (continued)								
C. Reform of marriage legislation				0	1		1	2
D. Accountability of home missions fund				0	1			1
E. Opposition to abortion legislation				0	1	1		2
F. Support of the rite of annointing for alcoholics				0			1	1
G. Rural ministry				0			1	1
H. Inter-cooperation with Catholic organizations				0		1	1	2
I. Public religious education				0	1			2
3. Alternative Ministries	2	1	1	4	6	2	1	9
A. Permanent diaconate	1			1	1	1		2
B. Research and implement alternatives	1	1		2	3			3
C. Study priesthood of married men			1	1	1			1
D. Support women ministers				0	1	1		2
E. Search and share directory				0			1	1
PERSONNEL	8	14	8	30	7	2	2	11
1. Accountability and Evaluation	1	6	4	11	3	0	0	3
A. Collaboration of parish clergy		2	1	2	1			0

Summary Table. *Resolutions passed at NFPC annual conventions (continued)*

	1969 N=32	1970 N=48	1971 N=31	1969-71 N=111	1972 N=62	1973 N=23	1974 N=24	1972-74 N=109
PERSONNEL (continued)								
1. *Accountability and Evaluation* (continued)								
B. Better communication among bishop, council, and clergy		4	1	5				0
C. Professional accountability	1			1	2			2
D. Elimination of stipends				0	1			1
E. Personnel boards			3	3				0
2. *Research and Development on Priest Distribution*	1	0	0	1	1	1	1	3
3. *Bishop-Clergy Relations*	6	8	4	18	3	1	1	5
A. Issues of communication and cooperation between NCCB and NFPC	1	6	1	8	1			1
B. Clergy issues and International Synod of Bishops	2		2	4				0
C. Issues re: position, selection, and tenure of bishops	2	2		4	1	1	1	3
D. Support of Black clergy caucus	1		1	2	1			1
COMMUNICATIONS	0	1	0	1	1	0	0	1
Issues re: NFPC News Journal		1	1	1	1			1

Summary Table. *Resolutions based at NFPC annual conventions (continued)*

	1969 N=32	1970 N=48	1971 N=31	1969–71 N=111	1972 N=62	1973 N=23	1974 N=24	1972–74 N=109
RESEARCH AND DEVELOPMENT	**0**	**0**	**0**	**0**	**1**	**0**	**1**	**2**
Approval of research projects and budgets				0	1		1	2
FINANCE	**2**	**2**	**3**	**7**	**3**	**1**	**1**	**5**
Issues re: assessments and budget	2	2	3	7	3	1	1	5
PRIESTS' COUNCILS AND LAITY	**2**	**4**	**0**	**6**	**2**	**0**	**1**	**3**
1. Pastoral Councils	*1*	*3*	*0*	*4*	*1*	*0*	*0*	*1*
A. Development of diocesan councils	1	1		2	1			1
B. NCCB-NFPC work on national council		2		2	1			0
2. Evaluation	*1*	*1*	*0*	*2*	*1*	*0*	*1*	*2*
A. Research on NFPC structure and effectiveness		1		1	1		1	1
B. Evaluation of structure and function of senates	1			1	1			1
CONTINUING EDUCATION	**0**	**3**	**0**	**3**	**2**	**0**	**1**	**3**
1. Sponsor spiritual life colloquium		1		1	1			0
2. Establishment of diocesan house of prayer and study		1		1				0
3. NFPC as education resource center		1		1				0
4. National meeting of education directors				0	1		1	1

Summary Table. *Resolutions passed at NFPC annual conventions (continued)*

	1969 N=32	1970 N=48	1971 N=31	1969–71 N=111	1972 N=62	1973 N=23	1974 N=24	1972–74 N=109
CONTINUING EDUCATION (continued)								
5. Implementation of studies on the priesthood				0	1			1
6. Task force on clinical pastoral education				0			1	1
CONSTITUTION AND INTERNAL AFFAIRS								
1. Changes in by-laws (e.g., affiliation)	**1**	**7**	**0**	**8**	**19**	**1**	**1**	**21**
2. Restructuring of committees and personnel	1	5		6	4			4
3. Urging of representation of deacons		2		2	10			10
4. Convention business and NFPC priorities				0	4	1	1	6

Questionnaire on Organizational Effectiveness and Evaluation Background Information

1. What is your Diocese? ——; Province? ——; State? ——.

2. What is your current major work assignment? (circle only one)
   1. Parish work; 2. Chancery work; 3. Health and social welfare; 4. Education (including seminary); 5. Other diocesan work (specify).

3. What is your present title? (circle only one)
   1. Pastor (administrator); 2. Associate (assistant) pastor; 3. Professor or teacher; 4. Chancery official; 5. Diocesan director; 6. Other (specify).

4. What is the location of your present work assignment? (circle only one)
   1. Rural area (under 2,500); 2. Moderate city size (under 50,000); 3. Urban area (over 50,000); 4. Urban area—inner city; 5. Diocesan wide.

5. Are you generally satisfied with your present priestly work? (circle only one)
   1. Yes;   2. No.

6. Are you generally satisfied with the leadership of your bishop and chancery officials? (circle only one)
   1. Yes;   2. No.

7. What age bracket do you fit in?
   1. 24–29 years; 2. 30–34 years; 3. 35–39 years; 4. 40–49 years; 5. 50 years or older.

8. What is the total number of priests represented by your council? (circle only one)
   1. Under 50; 2. 50–99; 3. 100–199; 4. 200–299; 5. 300–399; 6. 400–499; 7. 500–599; 8. 1,000 or more;

9. What is the highest ecclesiastical degree (theology, sacred scripture, canon law, etc.) and non-ecclesiastical (secular area) degree you have

attained (or are near to attaining)? (*Circle only one code in each column* regardless of the number of degrees obtained)

Ecclesiastical	*Non-ecclesiastical*
1. No degree completed	1.
2. Bachelor degree	2.
3. Master degree	3.
4. Licentiate (all but dissertation)	4.
5. Doctorate	5.

10. Generally speaking, from what type of family background did you come relative to the following: (circle one code in each column)

A. *Parent's education*

Father	*Mother*
1. College graduate or more	1.
2. At least high school grad	2.
3. Some high school	3.
4. Less than 8th grade	4.
5. Don't know	5.

B. *Parent's political preference*

Father	*Mother*	C. *Father's occupation*
1. Democrat	1.	1. Professional
2. Republican	2.	2. Managerial
3. Independent	3.	3. Other white collar
4. Other	4.	4. Blue collar skilled
		5. Blue collar unskilled
		6. Other

D. How would you describe your social, political, and religious views? How about your parents?

Social-political	*Self*	*Father*	*Mother*
Radical	1	1	1
Liberal	2	2	2
Moderate	3	3	3
Conservative	4	4	4
Ultra-conservative	5	5	5

11. We would like some information about your position in the local council and the NFPC. (circle one code in each row)

	Yes	No	Doesn't apply
1. Are you the president of the local council?	1	2	3
2. Are you an official delegate from the local council to this meeting?	1	2	3
3. Are you a member of the NFPC executive board?	1	2	3
4. Have you attended provincial meetings?	1	2	3

12. What type of council do you represent? (circle only one)
    1. A senate type (presbytery, etc.)
    2. An association type (conference, etc.)
    3. Religious order type
    4. Other (specify)

13. In your opinion, how important/influential have been the following problems in bringing you and your fellow priests together for the development of the NFPC organization? (circle one code in each row)

	Very imp.	Consider-able imp.	Little imp.	No imp.	Not certain
1. Lack of leadership among the bishops and pope	1	2	3	4	5
2. Celibacy	1	2	3	4	5
3. Lack of freedom to experiment with new forms of ministry	1	2	3	4	5
4. No realistic commitment of the Church to problems of race, poverty, and peace	1	2	3	4	5
5. Lack of consultation from the bishop's office regarding priest's life and ministry	1	2	3	4	5
6. Lack of adequate protection for rights and character of the priest	1	2	3	4	5
7. Other factors (specify)	1	2	3	4	5

14. How important, in your estimation, is each of the following factors for making the NFPC more effective organizationally speaking? (circle one code in each row)

	Very imp.	*Consider-able imp.*	*Little imp.*	*No imp.*	*Not certain*
1. Official recognition of NFPC by the bishops	1	2	3	4	5
2. Greater militancy re: critical issues facing clergy	1	2	3	4	5
3. A public declaration of loyalty and cooperation by the NFPC and NCCB	1	2	3	4	5
4. Other (specify)	1	2	3	4	5

15. Does your council have a contact man for each of the following national committees? (circle one code in each row)

	Yes	*No*	*Not sure*
1. Personnel	1	2	3
2. Communications	1	2	3
3. Role of priest	1	2	3
4. Justice and peace	1	2	3
5. Lay councils	1	2	3
6. Research	1	2	3

16. A. What is the number of *official* representatives (elected/appointed) in your council? (circle only one category
   1. 0–9; 2. 10–19; 3. 20–29; 4. 30–39; 5. 40 or more.

   B. How many committees does your council have? (circle only one)
   1 2 3 4 5 6 7 8 9+

   C. Does your council regularly employ parliamentary rules in its deliberations?
   1. Yes;   2. No.

17. *To what extent* during the past year has each of the following contributed to the working order of the NFPC? (circle one code in each row)

	A great extent	A good extent	A little extent	Not at all	Not certain
1. How well established are the routines of the follow-units of the NFPC?:					
1. National leadership	1	2	3	4	5
2. House of Delegates	1	2	3	4	5
3. Provincial structure	1	2	3	4	5
4. Local council	1	2	3	4	5
2. How *clearly* defined are the policies and regulations that govern the tasks between the above mentioned units of the NFPC?	1	2	3	4	5
3. To what extent would you characterize NFPC as a cooperative, smoothly functioning organization?	1	2	3	4	5

Below are a series of statements concerning *leadership influence* of the NFPC during the past year. Please indicate your evaluation of each one by circling one code on each line.

	Great deal	Fair amt.	Small	None	Un-certain
18. How much influence has the NFPC exercised on the following groups re: a change of thinking on co-responsibility of priests with the bishops?					
1. Your council	1	2	3	4	5
2. Your bishop	1	2	3	4	5
3. NCCB	1	2	3	4	5
19. How much is the democratic process followed in the following groups?:					
1. The over-all national leadership of the NFPC	1	2	3	4	5
2. Your local council	1	2	3	4	5

20. In general, how much *influence* do you
    think the following groups have on the
    way the NFPC is run?:
    1. The officers and executive board   1   2   3   4   5
    2. House of Delegates   1   2   3   4   5
    3. The Province   1   2   3   4   5

21. Generally, how influential do you
    think the following groups have been,
    in actual fact, in determining
    policies and action in your diocese?:
    1. The bishop   1   2   3   4   5
    2. Your local council of the NFPC   1   2   3   4   5

22. In regard to diocesan matters, does your council or its committees
    have: (circle one code in each line)

	In many areas	In some areas	None
(A) Legislative powers	1	2	3
(B) Administrative powers	1	2	3

23. *Organizational Change*
    (A)   In the *past year* has your council adopted any of the following
          changes?
    (B)   Has the NFPC in any way been an influence on these changes?
          (circle one code for each item)

	(A) Adoption of changes			(B) Influence of NFPC	
	Yes	Always had this	No	Yes	No
1. Revised constitutions and by-laws	1	2	3	1	2
2. Change of powers of the council from advisory to legislative	1	2	3	1	2
3. Shifted emphasis to programs in social action	1	2	3	1	2
4. Due process machinery	1	2	3	1	2

24. In your opinion, (1) do the NFPC leaders respond to the influence of
    the following?

	Willingness to respond		
	Yes	*No*	*Uncertain*
1. Suggestions from the local councils	1	2	3
2. Suggestions from the delegates	1	2	3
3. Pressures from the bishops	1	2	3

25. The next series of questions concern *consensus* with the NFPC. How much are you in agreement with each of the following aspects of the NFPC? (circle one number in each row)

	Strongly agree	*Agree*	*Disagree*	*Strongly disagree*	*Uncertain*
1. The objectives and policies of the NFPC	1	2	3	4	5
2. On the amount of authority allocated to the:					
1. Officers of the executive board	1	2	3	4	5
2. House of Delegates	1	2	3	4	5
3. In the deliberations of the following units, consensus has been reached on most major decisions:					
1. House of Delegates	1	2	3	4	5
2. Local council meetings	1	2	3	4	5

26. The following beliefs/norms are considered very valuable by many priests in the NFPC. Please evaluate them to the extent you find them personally meaningful. (circle one in each row)

	Strongly agree	*Agree*	*Disagree*	*Strongly disagree*	*Uncertain*
1. Freedom of individual's conscience	1	2	3	4	5
2. Guarantee against deprivation of one's reputation	1	2	3	4	5

3. The right to engage
in *lawful* dissent
to authority   1   2   3   4   5

27. *Communications of the Local Council*
We would like your evaluation concerning the communications in your
diocese and council. (circle one code in each row)

	To a great extent	Good extent	Some extent	Not at all	Uncertain
1. To what extent does your council communicate to the priests of the diocese the activities of:					
1. the local council	1	2	3	4	5
2. the NFPC	1	2	3	4	5
2. To what extent do priests of your diocese communicate their needs and suggestions to the local council	1	2	3	4	5

28. Below are a series of questions concerning the *internal unity* of the
NFPC during the *past year*. Please indicate how you *personally* feel
about each of these items. (circle one code)

	To a great extent	Good extent	Some extent	Not at all	Uncertain
To what extent do you feel identified (committed) to:					
1. tasks and aims of NFPC	1	2	3	4	5
2. tasks and aims of local councils	1	2	3	4	5
3. tasks and aims of your bishop	1	2	3	4	5
To what extent are you satisfied with the following:					
1. progress of NFPC	1	2	3	4	5
2. progress at provincial/ state level	1	2	3	4	5
3. progress of your council	1	2	3	4	5
To what extent do you feel					

the following have been
marked by a relative harmony:

1. NFPC at national level	1	2	3	4	5
2. Provincial structure	1	2	3	4	5
3. Local council	1	2	3	4	5

29. *Communication within the NFPC*
    As you see it personally, evaluate each of the following statements
    concerning communications. (circle one code)

	To a great extent	*Good extent*	*Some extent*	*Not at all*	*Uncertain*
1. To what extent are the communications networks adequate for coordination of national leadership, the House of Delegates, and your local council	1	2	3	4	5
2. To what extent is your council informed by the following:					
1. National leadership	1	2	3	4	5
2. National committees	1	2	3	4	5
3. To what extent does your council send information about its significant activities to the national leadership?	1	2	3	4	5

30. *General attitudes about the NFPC*
    We would like you to view the following series of statements. Please
    indicate the extent of your own agreement to each statement. (circle
    one code)

	Agree strongly	*Agree some-what*	*Disagree some-what*	*Dis-agree*	*Un-certain*
1. There is a great deal of indifference among council representatives re: the work of the NFPC.	1	2	3	4	5

2. The NFPC is probably the most important tool in bringing about change in the priesthood.　　1　　2　　3　　4　　5

3. There is a great deal of indifference among rank-and-file priests re: the work of the NFPC.　　1　　2　　3　　4　　5

4. The NFPC has helped in the understanding that respectful confrontation (dissent) with one's bishop is necessary for change.　　1　　2　　3　　4　　5

5. The rules of procedure of NFPC's organization are adequate for its functioning.　1　　2　　3　　4　　5

6. There is a great deal of consensus on the part of local councils on the goals of the NFPC.　　1　　2　　3　　4　　5

7. The NFPC has been sufficiently accountable to the House of Delegates.　1　　2　　3　　4　　5

31. *Goals and Performance of the NFPC* (for each item circle one code in each column)
    (A) in your opinion, on which of the following tasks, functions or goals does the NFPC actually serve? For each yes, answer
    (B) how important do you feel each is, and
    (C) how would you evaluate NFPC's progress regarding each?

	(A)	(B)	(C)
		Import. of	
	Actually	goal, i.e.	Actual
	serve	priority	progress
	Yes No	Very Not imp. imp.	Good Poor

1. To enable priests councils to challenge the bishops with a

common representative voice
regarding vital priestly concerns 1 2 1 2 1 2

2. To move away from intramural
problems of the priests and
dioceses and get involved
with the issues of poverty,
race, justice, and peace   1 2 1 2 1 2

3. To be an instrument of change
within the church by taking
steps to achieve such
things as:
  1. due process machinery for
    each diocese   1 2 1 2 1 2
  2. realistice and open
    discussion of optional
    celibacy on the part of
    the NCCB   1 2 1 2 1 2
  3. allowance for experimentation
    with new forms of ministry
    and life styles   1 2 1 2 1 2

4. To develop new professional
standards for the priestly work 1 2 1 2 1 2

32. To what extent do you feel you and your fellow priests generally possess the following attributes of a *profession* as compared to other professionals, e.g. doctors, lawers, etc. (circle one code on each line)

	To a great extent	Good extent	Small extent	Not at all	Uncertain
1. Depth of knowledge and skill	1	2	3	4	5
2. Personal responsibility for your work	1	2	3	4	5
3. Autonomy in decision-making	1	2	3	4	5
4. Professional code of conduct	1	2	3	4	5
5. A viable professional ass'n	1	2	3	4	5
6. Commitment to serving the needs of people	1	2	3	4	5

Bibliography

Abbott, Walter M., and Gallagher, Joseph (1966), *The Documents of Vatican II.* New York, America Press.

America (1970), 'NFPC meets in San Diego', 122 (March 28): 325–326.

—— (1973), 'From turmoil to accountability', 128 (April 7): 301.

Barton, Allen H. (1961), *Organizational Measurement.* New York, College Entrance Examination Board.

Blau, Peter M. (1964), *Exchange and Power in Social Life.* New York, John Wiley and Sons.

Bonnike, Frank J. (1970), 'The president's message: progress reported in meeting with bishops', *Priests-USA* 1 (December): 1.

—— (1971a), 'President's message: the facts about elections', *Priests-USA* 1 (June): 5.

—— (1971b), 'President's message: suggests Synod discuss justice, then priesthood', *Priests-USA* 2 (August): 5.

—— (1971c), 'Who is self-serving, NCCB or NFPC?', *National Catholic Reporter* 7 (May 14): 13.

—— (1972a), 'State of the Federation', *Priests-USA* 2 (April): 6.

—— (1972b), President to President, Letter (June 1).

—— (1972c), 'President's message: a few questions about priest shortage', *Priests-USA* 2 (June): 5.

—— (1972d), 'President's message on Roman document: asks reaction to insensitivity', *Priests-USA* 3 (October): 1, 6.

—— (1973), 'President's message: "We are a beginning of what is before us"', *Priests-USA* 3 (January): 5.

Caplow, Theodore (1964), *Principles of Organization.* New York, Harcourt, Brace and World.

Carter, Alexander (1970), 'Address to the NFPC House of Delegates', pp. 9–13 in: *Proceedings of the NFPC Third Annual Convention, San Diego (March 9–12).* Chicago, NFPC National Office.

Casey, Rick (1973), 'Two U.S. bishops' votes go against Vatican decisions', *National Catholic Reporter* 10 (November 23): 1, 6.

Castelli, Jim (1972a), 'New image emerging for NFPC?', *National Catholic Reporter* 8 (March 24): 1, 6.

—— (1972b), 'NFPC president finds: relations with bishops improving', *National Catholic Reporter* 8 (March 31).

—— (1973a), 'Better relationships urged: be accountable to women, priests told', *National Catholic Reporter* 9 (March 30): 3–4.

—— (1973b), 'NFPC takes steps to put accountability into practice', *National Catholic Reporter* 9 (March 30): 1, 6, 15.

Castelli, Jim (1974), 'U.S. charismatics build church ties', *National Catholic Reporter* 10 (July 5): 5.
Christianity Today (1970), 'Priests' union: talking tougher', 14 (April 24): 38.
Cogley, John (1973), *Catholic America*. New York, The Dial Press.
Commonweal (1968a), 'The troubled priest', 87 (February 16): 582–592.
—— (1968b), 'The troubled priest: an exchange of views', 87 (March 15), 714–717.
Conway, J. D. (1966), 'The rights of priests', *Commonweal*, 84 (May 6): 197–200.
Dollen, Charles (1970), 'NFPC at San Diego', *The Priest* (May): 59–64.
Donovan, John D. (1967), 'The dilemma of the Christian priesthood', pp. 115–126 in: *Clergy in Church and Society*. Rome, International Conference of Sociology of Religion.
Egan, John J. (1968), 'The pastoral ministry and life of the priest'. Private circulation. Delivered at a meeting on priests' councils, Des Plaines, Illinois (February 12–13, 1968).
—— (1971), 'Priest power in Baltimore', *Commonweal* 94 (April 9): 101–102.
—— (1974), 'Priests' councils: grounds for hope', *Commonweal* 100 (April 12): 124–125.
Ellis, John Tracy (1969), *American Catholicism*. Chicago, University of Chicago Press.
Etzioni, Amitai (1961), *A comparative Analysis of Complex Organizations*. New York, The Free Press.
Evans, Robert R., Ed. (1973), *Social Movements: A Reader and Source Book*. Chicago, Rand McNally.
Executive Board Minutes (1968), Los Angeles (December 9–11).
—— (1969), New Orleans (March 26).
—— (1970a), Chicago (August 30–September 2).
—— (1970b), Chicago (December 14–16).
—— (1971), Scottsdale, Arizona (November 30–December 3).
Fichter, Joseph H. (1968), *America's Forgotten Priests: What They Are Saying*. New York, Harper and Row.
Flaherty, Daniel L. (1968), 'Council of priests: a historical first', *America* 118 (March 2): 290–293.
Georgopoulos, B. (1957), The Normative Structure of Social Systems. A Study of Organization Effectiveness. Ph.D. dissertation. Ann Arbor, University of Michigan.
Gill, James J., SJ, M.D. (1973), 'Personal accountability'. Address to the National Federation of Priests' Councils, House of Delegates Annual Meeting (March 19).
Greeley, Andrew M. (1966), *The Hesitant Pilgrim*. New York, Sheed and Ward.
—— (1967), *Uncertain Trumpet: The Priest in Modern America*. New York, Sheed and Ward.
—— (1972a), 'The state of the priesthood', *National Catholic Reporter* 8 (February 18): 7–17.
—— (1972b), *The Catholic Priest in the United States: Sociological Investigations*. Washington, D.C., USSC.
—— (1974), 'Why priests stay', *National Catholic Reporter* 10 (April 12): 24.
Gusfield, Joseph R. (1970), *Protest, Reform, and Revolt*. New York, John Wiley and Sons.

Hall, Douglas T., and Schneider, Benjamin (1973), *Organizational Climates and Careers*. New York, Seminar Press.

Haughy, John C. (1971), 'The NFPC's celibacy stand', *America* 124 (April 3): 341–343.

Herman, Florence L. (1969), 'Federation head cites needs', *Clarion Herald* 7 (March 27): 1, 8.

Hill, John (1967), 'Priests' associations go regional', *Commonweal* 87 (October 20): 69–70.

—— (1968), 'National collaboration: a rationale'. Delivered at a meeting on priests' councils, Des Plaines, Illinois (February 12–13).

Joyce, John M. (1974), 'NFPC's goal: role in running the church', *National Catholic Reporter* 10 (March 29): 21.

Kennedy, Eugene C., and Heckler, Victor J. (1971), *The Catholic Priest in the United States: Psychological Investigations*. Washington, D.C., USSC.

Kennedy, Robert (1967), Unpublished research surveying diocesan senates.

—— (1968), 'Priests' councils: a review', in: *Proceedings of the National Meeting of Priests' Councils (February 12–13)*. Chicago, NFPC National Office.

Koval, John P., and Bell, Richard (1971), A Study of Priestly Celibacy. Unpublished Report.

Kung, Hans (1967), *The Church*. New York, Sheed and Ward.

LaPalombara, Joseph G. (1964), *Interest Groups in Italian Politics*. Princeton, N.J., Princeton University Press.

Landecker, W. S. (1955), Types of integration and their measurement', pp. 19–27 in: Paul E. Laxersfeld and Morris Rosenberg (Eds.), *The Language of Social Research*. New York, The Free Press.

Likert, Rensis (1961), *New Patterns of Management*. New York, McGraw-Hill.

MacEoin, Gary (1966), *What Happened at Rome?* New York, Holt, Rinehart and Winston.

—— (1971), 'Bonnike says: Synod evaded issues', *National Catholic Reporter* 7 (October 29): 5.

Maddock, L. (1972), 'Search for issues', *Commonweal* 96 (April 7): 102–103.

Mahoney, John (1973), 'The priests' councils: an unstable coalition', *Commonweal* 98 (April 20): 148–149.

Mannheim, Karl (1946), *Ideology and Utopia*. New York, Harcourt, Brace and Company.

Mayo, Reid C. (1973a), 'State of the Federation', *Priests-USA* 3 (April): 1–4.

—— (1973b), "President's column: right attitudes. Requisites for peace and harmony', *Priests-USA* 4 (August): 5.

—— (1973c), 'President's column: new style of leadership', *Priests-USA* 4 (November): 5.

—— (1974a), 'State of the Federation', Address to the National Federation of Priests' Councils, House of Delegates, Seventh Annual Convocation. San Francisco (March 19).

—— (1974b), 'President's column: goals as envisioned by president', *Priests-USA* 4 (April): 5.

—— (1975), 'President's call to assembly', *Priests-USA* 5 (April): 2.

Memorandum (1969). Addressed to the NFPC Executive Board by Patrick O'Malley (April 17).

Merton, Robert K. (1957), *Social Theory and Social Structure*. New York, The Free Press.

Millon, David (1971), 'NFPC chooses justice as convention theme', *National Catholic Reporter* 7 (December 17).

Minutes (1967). Unpublished minutes of an ad hoc meeting on national collaboration, Chicago (May 9).

National Catholic Reporter (1969a), 'Bid for "crucial issues" grabs spotlight', (April 2): 3.

—— (1969b), 'Priests to take disputes to church courts', (May 7): 6.

—— (1969c), 'Patrick O'Malley says he has "most positive" session with Archbishop McDonough', (March 26): 10.

—— (1970a), 'Priests want law-making shared throughout the church', (March 18): 1.

—— (1970b), 'Washington 19 puzzled by letter from Vatican', (May 29): 11.

—— (1972), 'Says need for NFPC still exists', 8 (March 24): 6.

—— (1974), 'Priests debate ministry to gays', 10 (March 29): 1, 24.

Neal, Marie Augusta, S. N. D. (1965), *Values and Interests in Social Change*. Englewood Cliffs, N.J., Prentice-Hall.

Nelson, Glenn I. (1964), Social Change in Rural Churches. Unpublished. Minneapolis, University of Minneapolis.

New Orleans States-Item (1969), 'Priests demand "due process": disputes with bishops cited', (March 26): 1, 6.

Newsweek (1967), 'How U.S. Catholics view their church', (March 20): 68–75.

—— (1971a), 'A priest is as a priest does', (May 10): 74–75.

—— (1971b), 'Has the church lost its soul?', (October 4): 80–90.

NFPC-NCCB Liaison Committee Meeting (1970). Minutes (August 20).

NFPC Newletter (1968a), 'Interview with Patrick J. O'Malley', 1 (July). Chicago, NFPC National Office.

—— (1968b). 1 (December). Chicago, NFPC National Office.

Novak, Michael (1964), *The Open Church*. New York, Macmillan.

O'Brien, David J. (1971), 'The American priest and social action', pp. 423–469 in: John Tracy Ellis (Ed.), *The Catholic Priest in the United States: Historical Investigations*. Washington, D.C., USSC.

—— (1974), 'Signs of Hope'. Address to the National Federation of Priests' Councils, House of Delegates, Seventh Annual Convocation. San Francisco (March 19).

O'Dea, Thomas F. (1968), *The Catholic Crisis*. Boston, Beacon Press.

O'Gara, James (1966), 'A union for priests', *Commonweal* 84 (April 8): 72–74.

O'Grady, Desmond (1972), '13,000 priests left over six-year period', *National Catholic Reporter* 96 (April 28): 3–4.

Olmstead, B. (1970), 'Priests near showdown on 'Washington 19', *National Catholic Reporter* 6 (April 24): 1.

O'Malley, Patrick (1969a), 'Executive's desk', *Priests' Forum* 1 (March/April): 15.

—— (1969b), 'State of the federation', *Priests' Forum* 1 (May/June): 11, 27–32.

—— (1969c), "Address of the President, National Federation of Priests' Councils,

to the National Conference of Catholic Bishops', *Priests' Forum* 1 (December 1969/January 1970): 7–11.
—— (1970), 'State of the federation', pp. 15–19 in: *Proceedings of the National Federation of Priests' Councils, Third Annual Convention, San Diego (March 9–12).* Chicago, NFPC National Office.
Osborne, William A. (1969), 'The church as a social organization: a sociological analysis', pp. 33–50 in: Philip Gleason (Ed.), *Contemporary Catholicism in the United States.* Notre Dame (Ind.), University of Notre Dame Press.
Padovano, Anthony (1970), 'Ecclesiastical authority and the senate of priests', *Chicago Studies* (Summer): 203–222.
Parsons, Talcott (1956), 'Suggestions for a sociological approach to the theory of organizations', *Administrative Science Quarterly* I(1): 63–85; I(2): 224–239.
—— (1959), 'General theory in Sociology', pp. 3–38 in: Robert K. Merton et al. (Eds.), *Sociology Today*, Vol. 1. New York, Harper and Row.
—— (1960), *Structure and Process in Modern Societies.* Glencoe, Ill., The Free Press.
Paul VI, Pope (1966), *Norms for Implementation of Four Council Decrees.* Washington, D.C., NCWC.
Perrow, Charles (1968), 'Organizational goals', pp. 305–311 in: David L. Sills (Ed.), *International Encyclopedia of the Social Sciences*, Vol. 11. New York, MacMillan Company and The Free Press.
Pin, Emile (1969), 'The priestly functions in crisis', pp. 45–58 in: Karl Rahner (Ed.), *The Identity of the Priest.* New York, Paulist Press.
President's Newsletter (1968), 'NFPC offers meeting with bishops in Washington, D.C.' (December).
Priests' Forum (1969a), 'Inner com?', 1 (March/April): 15.
—— (1969b), 'Executive's desk', 1 (September/October): 12.
—— (1969c), 'Year in review', 1 (December 1969/January 1970): 1–2.
Priests-USA (1971a), 'Proxies in Rome airing D.C. case', 8 (March): 1.
—— (1971b), "Delegates hear priest auditors to be at Synod', 1 (April): 1.
—— (1971c), '"The Moment of Truth"—NFPC statement on the priesthood,' 1 (April): 4–5.
—— (1971d), 'NFPC, bishops in dialogue', 1 (April): 1.
—— (1971e), 'Bishops meeting: many minuses, some pluses', 1 (June): 3.
—— (1972a), 'Justice, peace get priority', 2 (January): 1–2.
—— (1972b), 'NCCB committee names Bonnike', 2 (January): 6.
—— (1972c), 'Resolutions tell it all', 2 (February): 1.
—— (1972d), 'Delegates, back home, work on justice, peace', 2 (April): 1.
—— (1972e), 'Here are resolutions passed in Denver', 2 (April): 7.
—— (1972f), 'Notes from the bishops' meeting', 2 (May): 4.
—— (1972g), 'Canonists, theologians, others: out of harmony with new vision', 2 (June): 1, 3.
—— (1972h), 'Editorial: Is NFPC really timid?', 2 (July): 4.
—— (1972i), 'Justice and Peace Office: asks reflections on program proposal', 3 (August): 1.
—— (1972j), 'Editorial: NFPC/for better or for worse', 3 (September): 4.
—— (1972k), 'Progress reported in provinces, regions', 3 (September): 2.

Priests–USA (1921*l*), 'Denounce Vatican document', 3 (October): 1, 5.
—— (1972m), 'NFPC fights proposal', 3 (October): 1, 8.
—— (1972n), 'Reaction to rescript mostly unfavorable', 3 (November): 2.
—— (1972p), 'Improvement seen in bishops' meeting', 3 (December): 1, 4.
—— (1973a), 'Travelling symposium on investments', 3 (March): 1, 7.
—— (1973b), 'MacDonald to delegates: NFPC, NCCB must work together', 3 (May): 3.
—— (1973c), 'Mayo tells General Electric: pursue peace with plowshares', 3 (May): 1, 3.
—— (1973d), '"National collegiality"', 3 (June): 1.
—— (1973e), 'Task force on prison reform', 3 (July): 1.
—— (1973f), 'Clearinghouse set for resigned clergy', 4 (August): 8.
—— (1973g), 'Special report', 4 (September): 1.
—— (1973h), 'Analysis of bishops' meeting', 4 (December): 4–5.
—— (1973i), 'Mayo says: "valuable start"', 4 (December): 1, 7.
—— (1974a), '"Broad consultation" for office head', 4 (February): 1.
—— (1974b), 'Ambitious, hopeful', 4 (April): 4.
—— (1974c), 'Apostolic delegate to NFPC: other courses besides ours', 4 (April): 1.
—— (1974d), 'Many proposals face committee', 4 (June): 8.
—— (1974e), 'Mayo: rural workshop vital', 4 (July): 1–2.
—— (1947f), 'More NCCB progress', 5 (December): 1, 3.
Proceedings of the NFPC (1969), *Second Annual Convention, New Orleans* (*March 24–26*). Chicago, NFPC National Office.
Report (1967), Regional Meeting of Priests' Councils, Des Plaines, Ill. (September 25–26).
Roche, Douglas J. (1968), *The Catholic Revolution.* New York, David McKay Company.
Rush, Gary B., and Denishoff, R. Serge (1971), *Social and Political Movements.* New York, Appleton-Century-Crofts.
Seashore, Stanley E. (1965), 'Criteria for organizational effectiveness' *Michigan Business Review* (July).
Seidler, John (1974), 'Priest resignations, relocations, and passivity', *National Catholic Reporter* 10 (May 10): 7, 14.
Selznick, Philip (1948), 'Foundations of the theory of organization', *American Sociological Review* 13 (February): 23–35.
Shaw, Russell (1973), 'The alienation of American Catholics', *America* 129 (September 8): 138–140.
Sigur, A. O., Msgr. (1969), 'NFPC focus is on solid work', *Clarion Herald* 7(March 27): 1, 8.
Stewart, James H. (1969a), 'The changing role of the Catholic priest and his ministry in an inner city context: a study in role change', *Sociological Analysis* 30 (2-Summer).
—— (1969b), First Study of Organizational Effectiviness. Unpublished research.
—— (1970), A Career Model of a Professional Organization. A study of Organizational Effectiveness. Unpublished Master's thesis. Notre Dame, Ind., University of Notre Dame.

Stewart, James H. (1971), 'NFPC leaders and the rank and file. A study of constrasts', pp. 76–103 in: John Koval (Ed.). *Continuing Papers in the Study of Celibacy*. Chicago, NFPC Publication.

—— (1972), Second Study of Organizational Effectiveness. Unpublished research.

—— (1973a), 'Local councils still under-represented', *Priests-USA* 3 (July): 3.

—— (1973b), 'Values, interests, and organizational change: the National Federation of Priests' Councils', *Sociological Analysis* 34 (4-Winter).

Time (1968), 'Priest power', 91 (May 31): 58.

—— (1974), 'The new counter-reformation', 97 (July 8): 33–34.

Truman, David B. (1962), *The Governmental Process*. New York, Alfred A. Knopf

Turner, R. H., and Killian, L. M. (1957), *Collective Behavior*. Englewood Cliffs, N. J., Prentice-Hall.

Wallace, Weldon (1971), 'Backlash and the bishops', *Commonweal* 94 (May 21): 253–254.

Wills, Garry (1972), *Bare Ruined Choirs: Doubt, Prophecy, and Radical Religion*. New York, Doubleday and Company.

Wright, John (1970), Circular Letter on Presbyterial Councils. Vatican City, Sacred Congregation of the Clergy.

Wuerl, Donald W. (1970), 'Priests' councils', *Priest* (November): 7–16.